BEYOND TIME
New & Selected Work
1977-2007

Also by Robert Gibbons

Yellow & Black
The Woman in the Paragraph
Ardors
Lover, Is This Exile?
Of DC
This Vanishing Architecture
Streets for Two Dancers
The Book of Assassinations
Body of Time

Robert Gibbons

BEYOND TIME
New & Selected Work
1977-2007

Trivium Publications
Amherst, New York

Copyright © 2008 by Trivium Publications, Amherst, NY

All rights reserved

Printed in the United States of America

Requests for permission to reproduce material from this work should be sent to Permissions, Trivium Publications, P.O. Box 1259, Amherst, NY 14226.

Email: jhinfo@janushead.org

Cover designed by Bradford Fuller

ISBN 978-0-9713671-3-5

0 0 1 2 3 4 5 6 7 8 9 0 0

This book is dedicated to those fine, & small (using the word in this case to mean vast) press publishers who managed, somehow, often through self-sacrifice, to keep my work alive over a span of thirty years until this selection could be made: Dan Carr & Julia Ferrarie, Deborah Wender, Tim Miller, Claire & Victor Barbetti, & not least of all, Mark Olson.

As well as the more elusively named, "her" & "she," Kathleen.

Table of Contents

Acknowledgments   13

I. Beyond Time: New Work

Lifted Up	16
The Disasters of War	17
Goya Drew an Image	18
Swirling Palpably Around	19
When I Remember, & Move On	20
After Writing the Poem on the Soul	21
Suffused with the Light of a Music	22
To Pure Awe	23
Discordance	24
Rounding the Corner	25
When Love Cavorts with Time	26
Sky Told Him	27
Goya's Clenched Fist	29
The Tongue of Peace in a Feminine Voice	30
Orderly Arrangement	31
Time, Carved Out	32
A Mere Conduit	33
No Time at All was Lost	34
Time Allotted Here on Earth	35
To Other Lands, to Other Times	36
Such Venerable Space One Can Feel It	37
These Auditory Stimuli	38

Something Addressing Peace	39
We Fellow Americans	40
The American War	41
It's Veterans Day, What Now?	42
Under Cuban Sun	43
The Painting Speaking	44
One Word Dream Libretto	45
Even if He Read Them	46
It's Only a Matter of Time	48
Goya's Birth & Death	49
Shades Drawn Low	50
Anonymity of Time	51
Here, Just Here	52
Baghdad as the Origin of Writing	53
Out of the Vast Skies	54
Sudanese Women Waiting for Rations from the World Food Program	55
Carpe Noctem	56
"Why?"	57
The Eternal "Grrrrrrrrrr…"	58
The Gate is Open	59
Toward a Note	60
Blood Marks Time	61
April Cantata	62
Consonance of Time	63
Ahead of Time	64
Ancient Present Time	66
An Unknown Time	67
For No One, but Posterity	68

Beyond Time	69
When I Read Goya	70
Belief in Correspondences	71
Two Sides of a Mood	72
Where to Next?	73
The Goya Express	74
Going a Bit Out of My Way	75
Rose Up, Reaching Down	76
Reverencing	77
They Exited upon a Stage	78
April Fool	79
In the Words of Amiri Baraka at Mass College of Art	80
"Slaves weren't Allowed No Drums, So They Made the Banjo"	82
Goya Records his Fascination	83
Perhaps Some Were Decoys	84
Begin Practicing	85
Right on Time	86
Why We Want to Go Live with Wild Animals	87
Verging on Ecstasy, on Intimacy, on Raucousness, on Love	88
Goya's Sturdy Knifegrinder	89
Cross of Eternity	90
Mythic Tale	91
Beauty & the Beast Dream	92
Up for Air	93
Past Discarded Nets	94
Goya's Dog Today	95
For a Few Passing Moments	96
Eddie Vega	97

Sadui	98
Goat & Camel	99
Mouth of Time	100
On Marginal Way	101
Exchanges in Languages, Glances, Mask, & Doll for Self-Revelation	102
To the Hilt	104
The Dark Embers	105
At the Center of Art	106
The Handsome Face	107
Triptych of Time	108
The Aesthetics of the Fragment	110
Marble Stele of Kosmetes Sosistratos	111
Seventh Century Day	112
Triptych of Time II	113
Rembrandt's The Rat-Catcher	115
Philosopher in Meditation	116
Around the Edges of the Accusation	117
Dance of Time	118
Saving the Art of Dance	119
Black Spanish Wine	120
Quick Step	121
Time, & Time Past	122
Older than Time	124
Secret Snow & Fish Bones	125
This Thorn Tree	126
The View	127
Of a Stillness	128

Collision with Eternity	129
New Year	130
An Internal Chord	131
Trouble with Time	132
Time Guiding Her	133
Reversal of Time	134
Hauling Sunrise Rim to Rim	135
The Music of Time's Disappearance	136
Cudgels Fell There	137
Writing & Reading	138
At the End of Writing	139
Poetry & Death	140
Dirge	141
Oracular Time	142
The Death of Someone Close to Him	143
Time, Truth & History	144
Goya's Hungry Time	145
Why Jean Rhys Would Appear in a Dream?	146
Death's Graffiti	147
I Saw Time	148

II. Earlier Verse: *Stones Trees Names*

Name Painted on the Ceiling of the World	150
The Woman in the Paragraph	153
Love Also Creates the Mask	154
Light of a Dark River	155
Throw More Light	156

Rushes	157
The Dying Leaf	158
Exotic Birds	159
The Sturgeon River, or Merrimack	160
From the Usual Gentleness	161
Kouretes	162
Circular Angle	163
Photographing the Dream	165
Hearth	167
Big-Tree Night	168
This Morning on the Early Ferry	169
Ode to New York City	171
An Echo of the Silence of the Dead	175
If Blood Fuels the Engine	176
A Bruegel in Vienna for a Friend in Kiev	180
Cavafy's Men	181
Before Each Sacrifice	183
In North Lebanon	185
Providence	187
Stones Trees Names	189
Near Two Rivers	191
Border	194
Basquiat Never Babysat	195
Replenishings	196
The Three Trees	204
Amsterdam	205
Death as Intruder of Solitude	206
Cutler, Maine: Fruits de Mer	208

When Ivar Bardsen Gave his Chorography	210
This Afric Temple of the Whale	212
Past Ventry	215
Osiris	216
I Wanted to Get it Down: A Comparable Image	218
The Unmentionable	220
The Dream Bread	222
House of the Chaste Lovers	223
Nature or Civilization	225
There is a Fig Tree	229
Jade Cicada	230

III. from *Streets for Two Dancers*

Mass Transit	233
Boots & Divination	234
Communicating Vessels	235
Write Naked	236
White Dog (of Death)	237
The Good Dog	238
Precedents	239
Under the Spell of the Ballerina	240
New Moon	241
In the Arms of Two Black Shadows	242
The Only Open Ground	243
Dream Naked	244
Wanting to Speak	245
Discourse & Dialogue	246

Am I Ever More Ecstatic?	247
The Confusion	248
Dancer/Danger	250
Minutiae: Audience for the Dance	251
Confessional Poem	252
Our Portable Abode	253
One Day in the Same Vicinity	254
At the Foot of Wall Street, 1998	255
Pail for Ganymede	256
Lithe	257
Great Vehicle Body	258
Dream & Intoxication	259
It's Obvious	261
With Additional Light	262
This Vanishing Architecture	263
Prestige, from the French: Illusion, Trick, to Blind	264
The Little Band	265
Music of Venice	266
The Duality	267
Her Secret Recipe	268
The Little Phrase	269
The Present is the Roof of Time	270

IV. from *The Book of Assassinations*

The Woman & the Lotus	272
One Day, Discrete	273
Told This Way	274

My Violent American Way of Handling Things	275
Choreography of Desire	277
How Much More Alive Can a Man Be?	278
Keeping the First Heat of Summer Cool	279
Music	281
Large Tapestry	282
Grotesque: Half Bird Half Man with an Infant's Foot & Elephant's Hoof	283
The Play on the Body	285
Documents: Homage to the Body	286
To a Red-haired Beggar Girl	287
History of Tragedy	288
Émigrés	290
Far Worse than This Deadening Cold	291
That Face	292
As Quiet as One Can Get	293
Moment in Monument	294
About American Poetry	296
Perhaps I Went a Little Too Far	297
Another Key to the Dwelling	298
Distance & Absence	301
Serving the Sentence	302
Making Her Way	303
Practicing for the Big Trip	304
Chagall's Murals for the Jewish Museum in Moscow: Love on the Stage	306
Balboa Betrothed	308
The Premonitory Fog Walks Around	310

Walking San Francisco Thirty-Two Years Ago to the Present Moment	311
Preparations for San Francisco & Napa	312
The First Order of the Day	314
"Ah, Freedom"	315
For a Second there my Briefcase was a Leather Holster	316
Departure	317
Ordering the Waves	318
Jettisoned	319
Deep Association	320
Love & Time Equal to Snow	321
Yet Another Time to Love	322

V. from *Body of Time*

The Physical Universe	324
Headlines	325
A Small Stone	326
Close Reading	327
Purity & Mercy	328
Last Train to Montpellier	329
Breakthrough	330
Tear the Flesh of Language Open	331
Irrational as Animals	332
Torso	333
Woman Married to the Sun & Wind	334
Events Where They Should Be	335
The Boat in the Sky Sailed Past	336

Seaman's Identity Card	337
Time Ahead	338
Small Caps & Nasdaq Slip in Thin Trading	340
London Long Beach LA Watts Compton	341
Zen February: Coltrane Piece	345
Aegean Shimmering	346
Everything is Marked	348
Today I Want to Shape it a Bit Differently	349
How Far Back does Desire Reach?	351
How to Get it Out!	352
Self-Portrait, after Rilke	353
Learning Joyously Learning	354
The Man with Two Souls	355
Nativity with Dance	356
Convulsive Beauty	358
Drawings for Dante's Inferno	359
When Time is No Solution	360
To Breathe the Least Bit of Fresh Air	361
First TV Appearance	362
Simone	363
Can You Get a Sense of the Weight of a Gun from the Movies?	365
Elliptical, Cryptic Fragments Stand in for Entire Philosophical Tracts	366
In the Remotest Mansions of the Blood	368
That Most Melancholic of Bach	369
The Music & Art of a Friend in Vienna	370
On the Day that I Met Him	371
Toward the Center	373

Crossroads	375
Venice via Hell & Belgrade	376
A Last Reminder	378
Three Liberating Dreams	379
Diving through the Other Side of Time	380

Acknowledgments

"Seaman's Identity Card," was first published in *2River*; "About American Poetry" and "An Internal Chord," *42opus*; "Dream & Intoxication," *The American Journal of Print*; "In the Remotest Mansions of the Blood," *Ars Interpres, (Sweden)*; "Circular Angle," *Bezoar*; "Replenishings," *Cauldron & Net*; "Even if He Read Them" and "Under Cuban Sun," *Counterpunch*; "Around the Edges of the Accusation" and "The Aesthetics of the Fragment," *Double Room*; "Aegean Shimmering," "Another Key to the Dwelling," "Everything is Marked," "History of Tragedy," "How Far Back Does Desire Reach?," "Time Ahead," "To Breathe the Least Bit of Fresh Air," "Today I Want to Shape it a Bit Differently," "Toward the Center," "When Time is No Solution," and "Woman Married to the Sun & Wind," *The Drunken Boat*; "Small Caps & Nasdaq Slip in Thin Trading," *Electric Acorn (Dublin Writers' Workshop)*; "Purity & Mercy" and "Last Train to Montpellier," *Evergreen Review*; "Boots & Divination," "Communicating Vessels," "Confessional Poem," "The Good Dog," "White Dog (of Death)," and "Write Naked," *Exquisite Corpse*; "Match Point," *Frank: an International Journal of Writing & Art, (Paris)*; "Choreography of Desire," "Her Secret Recipe," "Keeping the First Heat of Summer Cool," "Love & Time Equal to Snow," "The Man with Two Souls," "Three Liberating Dreams," and "Yet another Time to Love," *Gargoyle*; "Providence," *Gavea-Brown*; "One Day in the Same Vicinity," *The God Particle*; "Close Reading," "Events Where They Should Be," "Self-Portrait after Rilke," and "Zen February: Coltrane Piece," *Jack Magazine*; "At The End of Writing," *Jacket*; "Dirge," "Elliptical, Cryptic Fragments Stand in for Entire Philosophical Tracts," "Sophia's," "Swirling Palpably Around," and "To a Red-Haired Beggar Girl," *Janus Head*; "At the Foot of Wall Street, 1998," "Breakthrough," "Diving through the Other Side of Time," "Distance & Absence," "Drawings for Dante's Inferno," "Grotesque: Half Bird Half Man with an Infant's Foot & Elephant's Hoof," "Headlines," "Mass Transit," "Minutiae: Audience for the Dance," "Simone," "The Only Open Ground," and "The Physical Universe," *Linnaean Street*; "Venice via Hell & Belgrade," *The Literary Review*; "On the Day that I Met Him," *Niederngasse*; "New Year," "Something Addressing Peace," and "Time Guiding Her," *Not Just Air*; "Dancer/Danger," *Pith*; "Such Venerable Space One Can Feel It," *Portland Press Herald*; "Belief in Correspondences," *Shadowtrain*; "Am I Ever More Ecstatic?," "Great Vehicle Body," "How to Get it Out!," "It's Obvious," "Music," "Nativity with Dance," "Precedent," "The Boat in the Sky Sailed Past," "The Confusion," and "The Woman & the Lotus," ***Slow Trains Literary Journal***; "That Face," and "The Play on the Body," ***Snow Monkey***; "Under the Spell of the Ballerina," ***Stirring***; and "Cross of Eternity" in ***Wheelhouse***.

"The Woman in the Paragraph" was published in the **Night House Anthology: 48 Younger American Poets**.

"Hearth," "Osiris," and "Rushes" first appeared **Yellow & Black**, a chapbook published in Boston by Four Zoas Night House Press.

"Exotic Birds," "From the Usual Gentleness," "Kouretes," "Love Also Creates the Mask," "Past Ventry," and "The Sturgeon River, or Merrimack" appeared in **The Woman in the Paragraph**, Cat Island Press.

"Amsterdam," and "Light of a Dark River" were published in **Ardors**, Innerer Klang Press.

"Music of Venice," "Prestige, from the French: Illusion, Trick, to Blind," "The Duality," "The Little Band," "The Little Phrase," "The Present is the Roof of Time," "This Vanishing Architecture," and "With Additional Light," were included in the chapbook, **This Vanishing Architecture**, published by Mark Olson at Innerer Klang Press.

"An Unknown Time," "Beauty & the Beast Dream," "Beyond Time," "Blood Marks Time," "Dance of Time," "Here, Just Here," "I Saw Time," "No Time at All was Lost," "Oracular Time," "Reversal of Time," "Time Allotted Here on Earth," "Time, Carved Out," "Time Guiding Her," "To Other Lands, to Other Times," "Trouble with Time," & "When Love Cavorts with Time," were included in the online chapbook, **Beyond Time**, published in Dublin by Andrew Lovatt.

I. Beyond Time: New Work

Because as soon as one is in time, one sees that it is not what goes by but what stays, what opens itself. - **Helene Cixous,** *Rootprints*

*For each of you had an hour, or perhaps
not even an hour, a barely measurable time
between two moments -, when you were granted a sense
of being. Everything. Your veins flowed with being.* - **Rilke,** *Seventh Elegy*

Ever since I was twenty I've been doing nothing other than explore philosophers on the subject of love. - **Jacques Lacan,** *Feminine Sexuality*

Human labor resurrects things from the dead.
— **Jean-Luc Godard,** *Masculine Feminine*

To render Time sensible in itself is a task common to the painter, the musician, and sometimes the writer. It is a task beyond all measure or cadence. - **Gilles Deleuze,** *Francis Bacon: The Logic of Sensation*

But knowledge, in taking up a datum, is also a refusal of the datum. The datum does not exclude just possibilities. It is drawn – abstracted – from the totality of the real that stretches endlessly beyond it. It is as if knowledge moved beyond the datum, without having to gauge the height or degree of that beyond.
— **Emmanuel Levinas,** *Alterity & Transcendence*

Lifted Up

I walked alone, on purpose, under the giant crane renovating the mansion on Danforth only out of superstition, like a dream, or rain falling intermittently on this yellow pad blotting the ink here & there, or the miracle of shimmering dahlia petals, lips speaking next to me in the wind, my strange superstition connected to the use of *deus ex machina* on the Roman stage, by which it introduced the god to the scene, in order to intervene, or to remove the hero from danger, hoping, one might say, that I, too, could be lifted up, beyond mere potential of the poem, or sentence, & somehow, by some spirit, put to good use, as a man.

The Disasters of War

Terror goes a long way, spawning trauma at the depths of living. However, transformed in that dark undercurrent, in dire circumstances, at the bitter end of a long ordeal, the whole enterprise can turn around, reverse the fear. Two examples come to mind from *The Disasters of War*, which didn't see the light of day for thirty-five years after Goya passed away. In "What Courage!" a young woman climbs over battlefield dead to light the cannon against relentless onslaught. In 'They Do Not Want To,' an old woman's dagger is the exclamation driving home the point written quietly in pencil at margin's edge. Perhaps it's just that man has to earn courage, woman's is more innate.

Goya Drew an Image

Goya drew an image just as we do a breath. Unfairness, torture, gossip, calumny, poverty, war, pride, butchery, ignorance, disregard, weakness, he drew human frailty & fallibility in perpetuity. To the extent that his "Beggar with a Cane in his Right Hand," didn't even bother to stand today, sitting on a muddy bank in the sun with a scarf & a hundred layers on, & not bothering to beg, because one thing that *has* changed is this age's disbelief in charity on a small scale. Forget giving alms directly to the poor, it has to be on some grand, elaborate scale, tax-deductible with all the receipts & paperwork organized, when the lawyers ask.

Swirling Palpably Around

We made this sort of jagged parabolic trek out State Street, back around Stetson Court to Park, down Congress to the Yoga Center she wants to join, around High down to Sturdivant's Wharf. I spotted the *Seneca* out of Boston across the way, a long-liner to the best of my knowledge, & next to it the *Snow Squall*, a beauty of a large white lobster boat tied up to it. The Asian guy with his fishing rod mimicked the top end of a pier pole standing invisible to both of us until I caught sight of him & had to point him out for her to see. Getting to the end of the wharf was a gauntlet run past workers on smoke breaks, & toxic marine paint applied to a number of hulls up on dry dock, but it was all worth it when the *Déjà Vu II* rolled in near the *Snow Squall* with one of the crew yelling out asking if they wanted some good bait. The two guys on the *Snow Squall* were apprehensive at first, but the loquacious lobsterman on the *Déjà Vu* talked up the bait for all it was worth, & free, after all. One of the guys finally nodded & the whole plastic vat passed hands. But the captain wanted the lug back, so one of *Squall's* crew tossed the contents into one of his own. That was it! A stream of Silver & Gold shining in the sun, hundreds of beautiful, free herring flashing in the sun! Miraculous, in a simple sort of way. After one crew member emptied the tub he handed it over to the guy who'd nodded acceptance, who then graciously washed it out in harbor water before handing it back to the talkative sailor still talking, the spirit of generosity swirling palpably around the whole area like a nimbus.

When I Remember, & Move On

I spent the day alone, dutifully, as word & law required. Among all my flaws one could say. That healthy recognition. Breath slowed, eyes strengthened to observe shadow of tree before the tree, color & distance of sea before the sea. A certain resolve in knowledge of the self that needn't return there for long, but remember, & move on. Remember, & move on, so that shadow & tree, color, distance & sea will accompany me, when I remember, & move on.

After Writing the Poem on the Soul

Went for a walk after writing the poem on the Soul, where I saw the fox, a fox at the end of the earth, ten feet from the seawall, just out from under the deck of the oldest summer house, a truly summer summer house with two second-floor windows boarded up, sashes having given way at the first bad weather in the fall. Thrilled to see the adolescent female, which took my compliment that she was beautiful (saying it aloud without missing a step in my gait past ramshackle 143 Turner) curling up & lying down in the sand, more like a cat, than a canine. Whereupon, on the trek home I ruminated about writing that poem about the Soul, when in fact it was all about the Body.

Suffused with the Light of a Music

for **Patricia, Pablo, & Xavier**

They could have charged extra back then, when I boarded the plane in Belgrade, for the extra weight of my ignorance. But we took off without a hitch, leaving sad green metal drums of communism behind for the laissez-faire light of Venice forty years ago next summer. Glorious memories flashing on & off & often like ripples on larger lagoons or leaded stained glass over smaller canals. Contrast of darkness & light emerged again recently, when a woman from The Art Institute of Chicago entered the confines of my work area with her young son, Pablo, all of eleven, violin tuned, sheet music set up in front of the Chinese lamp in order to play Vivaldi's *Concerto in G Minor*. Suddenly, space suffused with the light of a music I was surely deprived of at his age, hearing him now turned the drudgery of my hourly wage into privilege & gift more closely resembling that offered up to one of the Bellini Doges.

To Pure Awe

Sensitive enough, light gives off burning edges of fire, or voice an extended aria. When touch is nothing but love, death gets erased: an accomplished impossibility. Life has moments filled with this music. Woke to her three different, magnificent times already. It's only midweek. Never thought I'd get this old, nor remember youth with any tincture of affection. Her eyes are proof of Rilke's angelic orders. Dig this. Talk about luck, fulfillment, chance, practically the equal, or better than winning at blackjack in Monte Carlo, (which I rode past fast in a silver Lancier, driven by an Italian I couldn't understand, when I was twenty): shook hands with a man this week who played bassoon with Stravinsky! My language changed in the falling interval to a deep breath, & rose, again, to pure awe in the progression.

Discordance

We purchased a recording by an unknown local musician on our first free day in Portland. It's soothing as a soothsayer, if a soothsayer is, which isn't likely, given the difficulty of transcription. The piano rings. "Look," I said to Joan White, then apologized. Why should I say "look" to someone, when she's already paying attention? You'll never catch me saying, "listen" before I say anything. She was right about the university bordering on Roxbury, Massachusetts. She typed up Maya Angelou's poem for Bill Clinton's inaugural, read the day after we heard McCoy Tyner on the Mall. I'd want this string of sentences to end as atonally as possible, plunked down at the far end of the keyboard, discordantly, by the lovely doctor we sat across from at the picnic table, the one with just a few hours in town with his wife of a year & a half before the cruise ship headed off to New Brunswick, the one with three fingers missing from his right hand so that he shook goodbye with his left.

Rounding the Corner

Peripatetic I called myself, when she called me at home to make sure I got there all right, what with my continued refusal to buy into the American second-car in the driveway syndrome, refusing insurance for any other vehicle other than my body, & even that is only catastrophic. Otherwise, I'm free. To roam. Scope things out. Check damage from the recent storm, which Captain Dunbar tells me carried eighty-one-mile-an-hour winds across the harbor to Cape Elizabeth. Plenty of trees down, where one can peek under root boles for complexities & old stones. In my trek through town I stopped off at Micucci's for some cheap, but good Italian wine. Anna was hanging just about everything she could out of her halter top as cashier near the back door. The equivalent of four bottles of wine for under $15. Further on I stopped into Rabelais, the new bookstore on Middle Street, where Samantha & Don Lindgren have been open for exactly a week. My purchase of a first edition from 1960 of *Gastronomic Tour de France* went a long way toward bringing back memories of Nice in '67 & Cannes in '94. Told them so in just so many long-winded words! Don knows the meaning of "trivium," Samantha has a face filled with grace. The bus on Elm was filled with the usual suspects, along with a couple of young women who could have been in the dream last night I told Kathleen concerned "my Nicoise entourage," a half dozen women from Sweden, Germany, France, & the States. It was all good in the dream, & perhaps because of that, on the bus, as well. Got out early, trekking a few extra blocks to the house, where I opened the wine, put on *Shifting Down*, that brilliant collaboration between Cecil Taylor, Coltrane, & Kenny Durham. That's me, very peripatetic, no car, shifting down, no brakes, rounding the corner home.

When Love Cavorts with Time

Love cavorts with Time. When walking mid-winter in the late afternoon, straight toward sun at low level, she commented that light playing upon the architecture soothed her, as if the moment were an instrument, & brick & mortar danced. Loose-limbed, then, & sung along to, Love cavorts with Time. Nighttime craving its own light called full moon up from watery digs. Cyclical & rhythmic, then, Love cavorts with Time. In dreams, too, light pervades pitch darkness. Erotic & chaotic, then, reaching toward otherworldly realms, Love cavorts with Time. Perfection is not out of the question, then, when Love cavorts with Time.

Sky Told Him

Transported by more than public transportation, when with three bags of mine hanging from the wrought-iron fence surrounding the library parking lot on Elm across from the so-called bus station, which is nothing more than a sidewalk, a few awnings, along with posted schedules, & ludicrous maps, I hear, "Are all those bags yours?" "Yes, they are," I answered the guy with the long, jet-black hair & whitest of white women on his arm. "Are you an American?" he asked, responding to my nonchalant, unintimidated smile. "Yes," I answered, not yet getting the full nature of his query. "I knew it as soon as I saw you, something in the sky," pointing & looking upward, "told me we were brothers. I'm a full-blown Navajo, my father is a [Navajo word for it] you know, medicine man." Whereupon he gave me the arm & arm handshake, & hug.

"I'm a poet," I told him, "which is why we're brothers. What's your name?" which he told me in English, then Navajo. Every time he spoke in that language, what with his proclaiming that the sky told him we were brothers, I seemed to understand the words: the awe & authenticity. "I'm going to give you a copy of my book," which while I dug into the black canvas shoulder bag, he says, pointing to her, "That's Josie, you know, from *The Outlaw Josie Wales*." "Sure, I was just writing about the time I saw it at the 1994 Cannes Film Festival, just finished the piece today." He believed me, for the most part, but you know how things are on the street, so he told me they call him, "Chief" on the street, & of course, she was skeptical as hell, until I signed the book, & handing it over she asked my name. He pointed to the cover, reading it aloud at the same time I answered, grounding the three of us, & sending some sort of previously unheard, or newly resurrected chant + tonal caesura in the look the three of us shared, before they headed up toward the wilderness of Congress Street.

Goya's Clenched Fist

Invisible, internal, black bruises have much to say of dirt & blood. No surprise, that Lorca populates a tavern in Cadiz with Spanish ranchers & ancient men, who sacrifice bulls. This audience, waiting to hear Andalusian singer, Pastora Pavon, (whose voice the poet compares to Goya's clenched fist), has mud on its boots, & blood in its eyes. These aficionados know the bull must be wild as bitter wind when entering the ring it sees a man on his feet for the first time. Nothing less than that from the sound of his singer's voice, more primal cry than musical note.

The Tongue of Peace in a Feminine Voice

There is war. There is the girl in the yellow slicker riding her bike in the snow with her faithful dog on a leash looking up to see what to do, where to go next. There is always war, we must know that by now, which doesn't lessen the need to halt this latest. If powers of perception saw the moment's movement, the new. Two white houses across the street just changed color in the snow. Rhododendron exhilarates the universe, while war wounds unfathomably, to depths out of reach of photosynthesis, where everything stays white in darkness. Sounds familiar. Bullet in the backyard sounds, where war exterminates music. When I saw Miles perform in 1969 his anger was silent in blue & black. When I heard Munir Bashir for the first time on his Baghdad six-string ud, it matched the tongue of peace in a feminine voice. In her book, *Rootprints*, Helene Cixous says the world will ultimately forgive everyone, but war criminals.

Orderly Arrangement

No, open. No, open. An internal argument in progress, when Ruth Rollins comes back from her daily walk emptying a handful of chickweed onto my desk in order to show the difference between it & stalks of chicory she had sticking out of her backpack, which I kept pointing at yesterday, as she turned round & round, thinking I was pointing to something out the window, so many windows there in the lobby surrounding her perpetual pirouette, to the extent that I wanted to turn what she knew as supplement for coffee in her native Germany before the war, (before escaping the Holocaust), into a kind of laurel or wreath or award for her goodness as Mr. Emerson & his son George imbued the Alan sisters with in the Pensione Bertolini in Florence in *A Room with a View*. Cornflowers, the Englishmen called the blue bachelor buttons, not quite chicory's equal, & so far away from the darling, little, white flowers she placed in a tangled fistful on the desk, which I still saw orderly arrangement in before she exited the floor stage left.

Time, Carved Out

Green olives on a grey day, whose trees wave in the back of the mind. Leaves with silver dust reminiscent of an earlier journey in life, or current longing for a friend's return: hills of Cinque Terra. Black canvas bag filled with books, & a jam jar of red wine the only company at the moment, surrounded by free time, carved out the hard way. I believe in gravity as an asset to man. Leaves fall, olives burgeon heavily, instead of taking flight. On the ground by the tree trunk's roots, two fish-shaped stones wander in the direction of the sea as resolutely quiet as this solitude.

A Mere Conduit

Sun barely up this morning, sea smoke billowing past the Casco Bay Calendar Islands, right up to meridian's edge, a cross between sweet orange & faint pink, which only Matisse, or maybe a bit earlier Renoir could name the color of, surely not listed on any palette chart, but alchemically concocted in pursuit of color expressing meaning. This sweet orange mixed with faint pink rising out of the sea in air colder than the ocean soothed the senses & the heart, as if some brief childhood contentment sought a resigned old age, that I haven't reached yet, leaving me standing there in awe, a mere conduit for a forgotten Time reaching out to an unrealized Time, riding pulse & sensation of a color I'll call for now, Atlantic Saffron.

No Time at All was Lost

It was a lusty last hour of summer just ahead of the autumnal equinox. The sun pressing down hard on the inhabitants of our new city, when I dropped off a couple manuscripts at the post office, one guy drove up bare-chested on his motorcycle flashing an excellent tattoo replica of that self-same star. On the way home a woman walked down State dragging a mane of hair so long her head bent back as if under pressure of a tumpline. Way too beautiful out, I skipped the brown-bag noon-time lecture at the library hightailing back home to get her down to the eastern end of the wharves where abandoned pilings at low tide look like rows of Chinese soldiers uncovered thirty years ago in Emperor Qin's tomb. When we drove in, the shipyard workers on their half-hour lunch break couldn't take their eyes off her. The *Polar Adventure* out of Long Beach, California towered over the cruise ship *Realm of the Sea*. We counted down the minutes toward the equinox at exactly twelve-thirty, then the seconds, as small as anchovy bones, making that much the most of summer, so that no time at all was lost.

Time Allotted Here on Earth

Based my denial of Hell upon its ubiquity here on earth. Holocaust, war, famine, corruption of power, & the entire chain of subtler, personal circles further diagnosed by Dante. The belief that Hell is so much with us, there's no need to extend it after life. The recent dream, however, presented a different possibility. A woman propped up at the edge of a precipice, offering two bottles of wine, & then in a magic slight-of-hand hid one, possibly behind her back. When I got closer to the abyss to check around to see, I tottered in vertigo looking over the edge, suddenly entranced by the performance going on below.

The Beijing Opera Company (the dream said Peking) performing *The Wandering of Souls*! Stage set magnificent with trails & snow-topped peaks, valleys, lakes, & a huge, stone-carved fish (scales of the Carp of Good Fortune)? All, I assumed, constructed out of *papier-mâché*, or some other other-worldly material. The vastness of the cavern below accentuated by a lone Soul, head bowed, draped in a long, black cloak. Ancient poet wandering around the stage over the same winding paths composing interminably, (the only reason ever to want to wander again), what he'd wished to have accomplished during his Time allotted here on Earth.

To Other Lands, to Other Times

Those difficulties, these reassurances. Somewhat interesting in that I watched him watch her, who watched me watch without him knowing. They'd spoken in the café. Her with slight Asian accent. Him with straightforward American, paying just enough attention over his laptop. They timed a rendezvous between her cell phone & his computer. When she crossed the crosswalk she looked over her shoulder at him, at me, as I watched all three. Then, after glancing down at the front page of the newspaper with fires in Spain & floods in Switzerland, she'd bent over a good-sized granite stone in the park across the street, left foot lifted upon it, back turned contorted down to fix a sandal. Nothing in the paper, surely nothing he looked at on the screen could have been as transmogrifying to other lands, to other times. Only this fiction.

Such Venerable Space One Can Feel It

She'll go off, whether just walking, or teaching her students to relax, helping them find a more meaningful spiritual path through deep breathing & yoga. Fending for myself is fine for a while, but ultimately the gulf between us opens like the Casco Bay Bridge this morning, (taking note of it at exactly 10:10), which time had direct connection to her, every thought & longing for her lined up like cars & trucks I saw on the Portland side. There's a place, though, up in the loft, where her daily practice has carved out such venerable space one can feel it. It feels like her: gentle, resigned, amenable to all positive energies in the universe. A good place for me, who's the opposite in so many ways, honing in on the static, the chaotic, the negative, & attempting to reform that noise, again, through physical effort, less than spiritual, downright vulgar, in fact, trying to dredge up mud & dirt of words from underground, that hot lava & cold tufa of language that may result in early autumn dahlias, those hardy ones so clean in the rain out there on the balcony, balancing on sturdy stems, deep maroon & white standing against the grey today.

These Auditory Stimuli

Silence turns into a form of language, given her mere physical proximity. Reverberating, circulating, pulsating, but silent, nonetheless. Then she says, "I heard the breeze blow through the birches while teaching yoga this morning." I start hearing the beat of butterfly wings. Then Maxine comes down to the desk to report with a certain amount of astonishment & awe that Osawa conducted Mahler for over an hour & a half without interruption under stars & perfect weather at Tanglewood over the weekend. With all these auditory stimuli, I recall, & can't help reading a certain visual music into Kathleen's appearance in the dream last night, covered as she was with tattoos, the visceral score written into her skin.

Something Addressing Peace

A friend I met only once asked by letter today for something addressing Peace. At first I thought of lupine hiding in the mist at the side of the road on my way to work before six in the morning. Extremely humble, they seemed past their prime, but merely slept, waiting for the sun to show. Then, after putting in honest hours of manual labor here in Maine, I thought of the logging truck heading north on the highway toward the sawmill. Thoreau's probably the appropriate source in this context, distinguishing between the settler who can fell & grub up forest, make a stump speech, & vote for president on its ruins, but can't converse with the spirit of the tree he cuts down; can't read the poetry & mythology which retire as he advances. Now, Peace is surely an elusive thing. I've found it next to standing pines or redwoods, inside cabins & mansions. It may be all about what the external surface of things is willing to display, say five new peaches on the plate my wife brought home with immediate flesh less known than kernel hearts. We & all the others are the same way, having to dig deep down, drill new wells inside ourselves each & every Time.

We Fellow Americans

That lone fact, his look of a scavenging rat in the doorway on Tremont Street in Boston, made me suddenly turn back, having already shook off his request for "Change," realizing no one else was going to stop, & dropped the bills from my pants pocket into his plastic cup. His demeanor turned immediately into that of a fallen angel telling me how generous I was, & sending blessings my way. Kathleen said she saw him grab his gear right away, speculating he could now go sit somewhere, legally, out of February's harsh realities. I mean, after all, here we'd spent the night in the hotel's king-size bed, eaten wild boar & sea urchin roe at one of the best restaurants in town the night before. We'd just tipped our hat to the mayor of the city perched in the passenger side of a warm SUV waiting for festivities to begin in Chinatown. Way, way too many anachronistic details vortexing toward the visage of a man in so much agony, we fellow Americans could almost fool ourselves into thinking he'd somehow become used to it. Kathleen blurted out something about the lack of empathy of the rich, letting her voice trail off at the futility of even trying to link the two notions in the here & now of the pitiful condition our contemporaries are ready to leave the world.

The American War

In *Apocalypse Now* the beat of blades of helicopters could well match that of the Jimi Hendrix Experience, but instead Coppola begins with "The End" by The Doors, the very gates of Hell opening up. In his room in Saigon Martin Sheen's fan cannot cool him off, his body ends up, even there, bloody & naked, his image shattered in the mirror, hello America. Harrison Ford proceeds to give Sheen the order to terminate Kurtz's (Brando's) command with added caveat by innocuous CIA operator at dinner table arrayed with roast beef & shrimp, that it should be *performed with extreme prejudice, extreme prejudice*. Ford reiterates this mission never existed. When Coppola inserts himself into the film as an embedded television reporter he directs the soldiers forward as if they were really fighting. It's all theatre of war. Robert Duvall tags civilian dead with a deck of cards. No wonder the Vietnamese, among the most sophisticated of ancient cultures, call it The American War.

Apparently, obviously, relentlessly, without legal current ways to prevent them, we're not done deploying eponymous wars.

In whose name?

It's Veterans Day, What Now?

A night of dreams highlighted by a woman claiming to be a welder, & a man floating in the air. Welding? In some cases the weld is stronger than original material. What she meshed together could have been the iron railing we both leaned over for a better view of the sea, hers a dream sea, & my own real Atlantic with lone, black, unnamed tanker trudging into port. It's Veterans Day, when one more name is one more too many.

The man in the sky? Hovered there, fully dressed, feather on his head, another just visible above left shoulder. Not Icarus, but landing with ease to join a row of others like him, (he was young), roosting on the ridge of dream ground. What now? Some former platoon of soldiers, (they were always young), becomes a flock of angels?

Under Cuban Sun

> *An end to the granting of names, over you I cast my fate.*
> — **Paul Celan**, "Black"

Cuban sun. They sit in the wire-mesh cave of the Cuban sun. Maybe with a hood on in the black Cuban sun. In the cool of their senses shutting down the blue fish swim above & through detainees left to rot. I hear most refuse to speak with their lawyers, anachronistic term for any person representing someone where there is no law. No law no lawyer no need for dialogue. No centuries-old protection of habeas corpus against false imprisonment. There should be some difficulty here, there should be pain in writing these sentences just as detainees are held without sentences there is no language no Arabic no Farsi no Spanish, only American silencing. Lopsided & cock-eyed, the imbalance of judicial ruling in the case of Lakhdar Boumediene v. GWB, who surely never heard of Emmanuel Levinas, let alone his statement, "Peace as awakening to the precariousness of the other." There is no other to unbridled power. Shame visible in the scorched steel landscape of Guantánamo. Under Cuban sun. Shame reddening visible in the blood of all those who are other. No closed doors no end of centuries no

The Painting Speaking

Thought is made in the mouth.
-Tristan Tzara

Sun & ash. It's not that I refuse to allow the painting to speak for me, the painting which speaks for me, nor that, at this point, I am happy to be unknown. No, "Thought is made in the mouth," said Tzara, so out here in the open…

The politician pulls up to the meter, Jefferson takes a nosedive. Girl in red skirt outruns it in fear of what it may reveal. Child cries, inside. It's a morgue, then instant funeral. Someone mentions something about something hotter than the sun. I once had that dream about the monument long before seeing a photograph of it commemorating those lost at Treblinka. Blue sky filled with invisible particles. Clear blue? In front of Anselm Keifer's, *Sefer Hechaloth*, made of oil, straw, metal, & burned books on canvas, I was stunned that ashes had rained down from eight books onto the bottom frame jutting out for just that purpose. Upon return, months later, depths equally plumbed by the fact that some curator, or maintenance man, had swept them up, cleared the ashes away, apparently, without the least bit of ritual or ceremony. My vision automatically brought forth a row of open metal oven doors (mouths) of a crematorium, the painting speaking.

One Word Dream Libretto

What aspects led to it, how exactly the dream occurred the way it did in terms of imagery, sequence, sound, dénouement, & ending will remain mysteries, but surely, isolation on the island the day before, & knowing nothing of where things were or where we were going, other than following the paved road as directed by the first people we asked after disembarking, until the fork a few miles later, all contributed to the scene, but could never explain it fully. When we sat on the wharf level with the glistening Atlantic, I told her it felt like a dream, & then an unspoken comparison to both heaven & death shot past me faster than language. (For aren't sex & death & heaven beyond language?) We lolled there in the middle of time, time as slow & weighty, as to no longer be time at all, but living only, breathing only, sensing Nature having something beyond history, beyond any possible prediction for the future. Rock cliffs, stands of pine indecipherable as the expanses of cloudless sky, & depth of ocean. We must have stopped trying to figure things out: that night music filtered throughout the dream, solo stringed instrument, notes spirited, not droll, nor monotonous, almost jaunty in its rhythm, surely taken from some folk dance motif, when suddenly a lone word sounded from a male speaking voice: "Dachau............." Whereupon the music ceased immediately, & a silence became as palpably extended as those hours spent on the shell-sand cove at the furthest end of the island.

Even if He Read Them

For the second time this week the newspaper landed on our front lawn by mistake, as if trying to tell me something. Right now I'm as close to exiled from that world as I was in a small boarding house room in the center of Mexico City in 1974 waiting Nixon out, refusing to return here until that four-o'clock-shadow of an obstacle to Peace, that sinister thieving threat to Freedom left the grounds of the White House, straight up, forget the salute goodbye, commander! It happened at just about the Time I predicted it would, when a month earlier I practically chanted in the car we were in in Mitla with Manuel Avila Camacho, after he told me he & President Echeverria planned a State visit a few months later, "What? Nixon out in another month, Nixon out in another month, Nix…" Saying the name still grates on my nerves. Manuel looked at me like I was crazed, which I could have been, but wasn't, other than like a fox fleeing the hounds of a Republic that lost its bearings under two terms, under thumbs of thugs, under rugs. A Good Time. To be away. Certain presidents fall into this straight line lineage of bumblers, cads, ruthless bastards who read mass deaths as statistically as stock averages. So today, when the paper arrived with all the usual bad news I went straight to the sports, the comics, even read the horoscope I give no credence to, heading to the headlines last. But something of importance lurked on the bottom of the Obituary page below the society woman, who divided her time between Palm Beach Gardens, New York City, Dark Harbor, Maine, & charity work in Africa, below the former beauty queen & the Boston officer, across from Estelle Axton, Stax Records co-founder, there was Stanislaw Ryniak like a found poem with something to say. Warsaw-AP. First person imprisoned at the Nazi death camp of Auschwitz. Buried

February 20 at the Osobowicki cemetery in Wroclaw. No death date given. Arrested May 1940 in hometown of Sanok, southern Poland, accused of being a member of the Polish resistance. Arrived Auschwitz June 14, 1940 on first train of inmates. Numbers tattooed on prisoners' arms in order of arrival. First 30 numbers given to German criminal prisoners who would serve as guards. Ryniak's number = 31, making him the first inmate. Weighed, upon release in 1945, 88 pounds. Doubt our current president was proffered these statistics by his aides in the daily briefing this morning, holed up in the House he bought. Numbers that wouldn't add up to 1.5 million (people) dead, at Auschwitz alone, even if he read them.

It's Only a Matter of Time

Involved in a discussion, a political exchange, while imagining certain faces eventually sitting before a tribunal at Den Haag with its International Court of Justice located in the Peace Palace; the International Criminal Court; & the Organization for the Prohibition of Chemical Weapons. Didn't get specific, that will come. What I ruminated about, instead, was our own country, & possibly the world at large, bereft of the will to protest at mass levels that are able to touch even the foundations of those holding insuperable-invulnerable power at the top. It's only a matter of Time, of course, for "Time wounds all heels," but the damned meantime deals out & bodes forth such vicious rents in the body of Freedom, that trauma appears like a front page with coffee, & memory is delayed until beyond the grave.

Goya's Birth & Death

Don't want to know everything about him. Sure, let me place War & Inquisition in context, & a bit about the idiocy of Fernando VII, so that Goya's rendering of a featureless square block of stone standing in for the face of a king makes sense. Important to know the risk he took painting *La Quinta* walls with no assurance they'd survive the plaster. Exile, & why, to France. But as for the rest of the chronology? Just let me look! When dealing with the Eternal, even birth & death don't mean that much. For example, what good did it do to find out yesterday that Mahler died at fifty?

Shades Drawn Low

On & off snow flurries don't make me any less wary on the Ides. Intervals of clarity & sun won't lessen internal & historically-based trepidation. Current, shallow pols can't read potential tragedy into the day, how can they calling it victory? The middle of March is a window into the abyss of Time, shades drawn low.

Anonymity of Time

The grand anonymity of Time tree roots seek. The many more unmarked graves than graves marking history's plagues & famines, wars & genocides, extinctions & holocausts. Even Homer swore Odysseus ultimately longed for anonymity.

Here, Just Here

She walks away. Not away, exactly, but turns away. In turning a grace, in walking, a minor misstep as filled with balancing élan as the feminine is capable. A pocket full of quarters, she's simply heading down the hall with the laundry, but if some world traveler happened upon her halfway down there, he'd probably look around for this pristine Nausicaa's companions, surprised she's by herself. That first shy glimpse of her in a chapter some scholars theorize was added long after Homer chanted his version of **The Odyssey**, seems an incongruent, almost modern touch. It's not necessarily that I prefer it, the dirt surrounding the straps of Homer's sandals is the same dirt he washed down with wine to make his words clean. But here, just here, the masculine stink of ambition, avarice, & war, are nowhere to be seen.

Baghdad as the Origin of Writing

When I walk the seawall it's not like walking at all, it's flying, or total free fall. No physical energy expended. It's pure imagination. Hands & arms are wings. Head = engine. Legs treading geographical maps of D. H. Lawrence in Sardinia, Rimbaud in Africa, Walter Benjamin's Marseille. Today, I hit tide at dead low. Stones rose up near shore, & in the distance, some never seen before. Over my shoulder I looked for the full moon causing these new revelations, reminded that its light is part of the reason for the country's rush toward war. Thought of Baghdad as the origin of writing. Little cuneiform tablet, beautiful wedge, a work of art in its own right. 5,000 years old, mere grocery list, a receipt. But writing, nonetheless. I looked off in the distance to a walkway, a stone bridge, Charles Olson would have recognized, a phenomenon he'd phrase, *how, properly, to heap up*, allowing Algonquins (the word means "at the place of spearing fish & eels"), access by foot to shellfish beds without the need of dugouts. Women & children gathering food themselves.

Out of the Vast Skies

Fell on me like an infusion, physical rejuvenation, & spiritual validation, straight out of the vast skies of the unconscious of sleep underneath me, both words at the same time packing a light punch & heavy weight: GRACE BOMB!

Sudanese Women Waiting for Rations from the World Food Program

Hardcopy newsprint on the cover displays the color of Africa: Sudanese women dressed in traditional garb, striking yellow & black stripes, blue & pink grids, red & purple paisley trees, green floral patterns, without smiles cracking through their handsome, harried, desperate, earthenware faces waiting for rations from the World Food Program behind barriers of thorn branches. Chased out of villages by rival factions on horseback & camel, these are people on the infamous, other side of despair, too drained to shed a tear, too stunned to wonder past the misery of the present moment. The reporter writes, "An empty village is an eerie place. There are no babies crying, no goats bleating, no women pounding grain into mush." Seek it out, I don't want the underlying rhythm of these few sentences, my overriding concern for the narrative is no excuse just to write it. Do the research yourself, Tuesday, May 4, 2004, the whole Technicolor tragedy as hard to swallow, or stomach now, as breakfast.

Carpe Noctem

Black knife night. How easily the words fall down & out. It's as easy as betrayal. They say Joyce couldn't do without the idea, even to the point of imagining it, perhaps as means of ordering difference, or touching the Other. Much of Goya's oeuvre swirls around the black knife night of betrayal like a solitary piece of coal, or spilling black blood. Look at the ramifications of his *Disparate*, "Loyalty." It's a reminder of just how alive one can be, (alive to pain, that is), when the pinches, pricks, & taunts rain down as betrayals in the black knife night.

"Why?"

At first I don't know why, but then a stream of reasons flows, even for a man who doesn't believe in reason. Waking up with the word "carne" on the tongue? Hams hanging in a Madrid bodega? No, more likely human meat dispersed, & strewn over the battlefield in, "Bury them, & shut up." It gets worse. *Disasters* gets worse. The word "carnage" quickly follows under my breath, from the Indo-European, "to cut." In "What more can one do?" the man riven in two at the center of the splay of his legs by the soldier's sword is mercifully already dead. Which is more than can be said of the etching, "Why?" with its own agonizing intimations of castration. The defamation of corpses becomes too gruesome for any more words, except perhaps that of "carnival," at its root: "to remove meat."

The Eternal "Grrrrrrrrr…"

Eternal "Grrrrrrrrr……!" Listen, the eternal, "Grrrrrrrrr……" of disgruntlement & disgust of Goya coming our way, right there, close to the ground of *la Guerra*. In "Ravages of War," an anonymous hand is the hub of the wheel of chaos rolling, unrelenting, limbs of broken bodies swirling in the vortex of timbers of demolished houses, obscene spokes of splayed thighs & final cries, fallen silent & bloody & rank, yet rolling on with chairs balancing high in the air above crushed skulls of infants, nothing stagnant, whirling on, listen: the eternal "Grrrrrrrrr……" of Goya all the way up & down & beyond *Guernica*……

The Gate is Open

Never lose a holy curiosity.
- Einstein

Rembrandt & Ginsberg looking my way. Day of exquisite loneliness finally over, learned from. Come home to a rash of eighteen empathetic emails & snail mail from financers spelling my name wrong handing over the cash. I'm appreciative of every little thing. Read Williams's locust poem aloud looking at the real thing on top of Munjoy Hill. Woman walking with her striking daughter toward the Green Memorial African Methodist Episcopal Zion Church on Sheridan Street, Portland, Maine invites me in making me part of the larger congregation of the world. Defeat loneliness, if you can. Reach out. Hand out more five dollar Lincoln portraits to those in need. The gate is open to Etz-Chaim Synagogue with its spectacular image of the Tree of Life & wings of real evergreens straddling the long walkway on Congress Street dating to 3681.

Toward a Note

This singular sunrise. Dark curtain lifting. Dreams descending toward previous being, newly emerging. Friend's voice & brutal alarum. Sun whispering brushes across a drum. Distances cut in proximity to immediacy. Skin's movement: choreography of corporeal intimacy. Suddenly the ear becomes the center of one's universe, when a left hand reaches across the keyboard toward a note true improvisation refuses to know ahead of Time.

Blood Marks Time

Shut down the music as distraction; bring on silence for accompaniment. Such is the air of winter: spare, luminous, not fallow, but dormant, which given the nudge of elbow connected to nub of pen scratches ephemeral marks deep into the ice of the century. Suddenly seeing & hearing are one. Blood marks Time. Eyes become wings touching air, carefully enough to fly.

April Cantata

On a grey day the redemptive white page. Everlasting goodness of freedom on a day off keeping me away from the headlines. Grey gave way to snow on April second. First sighting of a robin with his look of embarrassment & disillusion, almost sulking, the poor bird, while here I was refugee from the rat race, no overcoat, but scarf & gloves, & no obligations, nor appointments, just the road, which wound down to Camden, where at the used bookstore three silver volumes of Proust kept behind the owner's desk matched the Bach Cantatas I drove the entire way with: a visual chorus. The guy had the look of someone who hadn't sold a book in ages, more downtrodden than the robin in snow. I gladly coughed up the twenty my wife left on the bed for me to get a good meal. I never lunch out anyway. What's another collection of Proust in the house, but influence on the redemptive white page, & everlasting goodness? The owner suggested the library as a place to access the World Wide Web, along with Zoot Coffee right there on the main drag. The reading room of the library is as rustically pure as architecture gets. Zoot has that quirky northern New England put-together amalgamation by folks on the fringe, & the best coffee outside my favorite café off rue Saint-Sulpice in Paris. There I was, again, inside of Proust's, *Overture*, where the taste of his lime tea matched my glance across the room to a woman's table with her clear glass cup surprising me filled with tea instead of coffee. The image added to my joy, while Proust himself, whenever he experienced involuntary memory in coincidence lost all fear, found joy, in correspondence between the present & recollection, lost all fear, found joy on the redemptive white page, where the everlasting goodness of freedom resides.

Consonance of Time

Calm sea & fog are one today. Horns reaching underwater warn clear-eyed creatures of brackish currents. Above the sea musical clangs & drones accentuate more deliberate shipping maneuvers. Waves drawn up to minor heights & keys & variations. There's consonance to the time where pilots full of concentration abandon laissez-faire ideas of commerce & competition to band together in communal caution & respect.

Suddenly the sound of voices on marine forecasts ring echoes of a Bach or Mahler chorus originally radiobroadcast out of Bremen, Hamburg, or Berlin.

Ahead of Time

Went out on the platform jutting right into the sea with sunglasses on I might ask them to bury me in, where I'm going, in this life paradise right before one's eyes. Spotting the tanker with a name I couldn't make out, I wished for someone like Bill Levandowski, who caught wild salmon in the furthest reaches of Quebec, & once drove precipitously down a road so hemmed in by snow & ice it might as well have been one-way for seven hours to get medicine his wife needed, knowing full-well he'd have a pair of good binoculars to catch the name. Moments later, he showed up, as if by sheer poet's will & desire. He agreed it was worth the trip, retrieving field glasses, & in no time walking out together, retracing previous steps, telling him I didn't need to look, but just for him to spell it out: T-R-O-G-I-R. White letters emblazoned on red hull, a mystery word.

Trogir, built in 1995 for the sole purpose of hauling diesel fuel, based in Malta. Told Bill about the time Uncle Ernie Provencher took me fishing as a kid, when I landed a brown trout first, but that when he hooked a rainbow, I claimed it as my own in tall tales to family & neighborhood friends back home, my first fish story.

After Bill helped me out with the name of the ship in similar avuncular fashion to Ernie's, I saw the *Trogir's* sister ship, *Tver*, with similar red & grey-green hull converging on the anchored *Trogir*. Now, at mid-thought in this attempt to steer around any shoals of nostalgia, I suddenly remember that when Uncle Ernie died I'd been away from home, & when his daughter called to ask if I'd carry the bier, I refused. Guilt followed me around in the echo of her shocked reaction. But today, with Bill's kindheartedness as bright as a wave's brilliant reflection, I realize, perhaps in the echo of the mystery words, *Trogir, Tver*, my uncle would have forgiven me, by loving him when alive, my denial, ahead of Time.

Ancient Present Time

That's a fishhook scar on the index finger of right hand typing. She greeted me at the front door after a full day's work at the factory, pouring a glass of wine accompanied by olives, cheese, & flatbread. Conversation spread far & wide, circling back to our own concerns. Balcony dahlias listened. Then, she said, "Look at that big boat," transfixed as I was on her visage, "should I get the binoculars?" When she left to get them, I turned around to see the huge *Patroklos* with its appropriate black hull, (after all, *he* wore Achilles' armor), flow downstream past the wide-open bridge with the agility it took to kill Sarpedon. Problem was Sarpedon was son of Zeus. We can all trace origins of tragedy, *afterward*. Sun kept afternoon at a steady seventy-six degrees, while shadows & shades plummeted toward unfathomable depths.

An Unknown Time

For that it is love and covers us out of all the ports.
-**Charles Olson**

Brief discussion, a loving one. About how time enters sculpture with Serra's new "permanent" installation filling up so much space in Bilbao. All that raw steel reminding me of the red-painted *barrera* surrounding the sand of the bullring. Then, in the middle of this conversation between loved ones, the *Vamand Wave* out of Cyprus blows into port. A beautiful, if-only-in-massive-girth-&-length- alone-oil tanker, decked out in fine gun-metal grey reaching down toward similar rust-red lower hull. I had just finished telling her Serra constructed a piece he titled, *Olson*, a long curved shank one could imagine the line the *Pequod* lumbered with over many seas. So here's the *Vamand Wave*, ambling in on June 8th, 2005, at 5:16 in the afternoon riding the same elliptical curve, as if sent from an unknown Time.

For No One, but Posterity

No question, alone. Why head there? The depth that Mallarmé's dice landed on with double sixes, the shipwreck. Somehow comforting, the death down there. All the homages at tombs of his heroes, Baudelaire, Verlaine, & his own son. Only Manet could portray the depth of that thought in paint, even Degas resorted to the camera to capture it, capture Soul in the mirror. So the poem gets written for no one, but posterity, which resembles cigar smoke & piano with a lone key out of tune. The "Z" Stevens saw as a man on his knees looking over the abyss.

Beyond Time

I thrive on these coincidences. Headed up to the sanctuary of the local art school library, where I can be alone with Rembrandt, Breughel, or even the Fluxus group with Joseph Beuys. Ultimately, though, I check out writers isolated against the back wall, behind their Dewey Decimals. Kafka, Kristeva, find **Frank O'Hara: Poet Among Painters**, & Knut Hamsun. A little gem of a red volume of Proust's last installment: **Time Regained**. Get home, open randomly to, *And so the cruel discovery I had just made with regard to the passage of Time could not fail to combine with all these other ideas and be of value to me in connection with the core and substance of my book*. What cruel discovery? Well, Proust first coolly places his discovery in an amusing fictive context, whereupon a young woman suggests they dine sometime at a restaurant together, & while the author agrees, he adds the caveat that he hopes she not mind being seen in public with a young man. Those within earshot laugh & snicker. He corrects himself. *I should say, with an old one*. This sudden, *cruel*, realization regarding the effects of Time on the Body jumpstarts his final ruminations on Time's ruins: his own body, & those of others. It's a significant lesson. One he feels most people ignore until the ravages of Time are visible, or felt. Proust skates upon the surface for a while describing the lines of Time on various of his contemporaries' faces, or in the lithe length of Gilberte's sixteen-year-old daughter, which he says is the measure of those same number of years already long lost to him. Then, finally, he dives to a depth of understanding only a writer of his caliber, obsessed with the nature of Time, could plumb, following the trail of Time's relation to the body to the extent that, *After death, Time withdraws from the body, & memories are effaced*.

When I Read Goya

Tasting freedom at the edge of margins. Delicate, fierce, delicious at the sword-edge edge between life & death. Back against the wall, open field ahead. Grand bullring life. In Madrid it's called *querencia*, where the bull feels right at home, an implacable space, which unless drawn out, the matador is gored. Writing a true sentence risks a life. When I read Goya, from crowded center of the canvas to inestimable edges of the frame, I find a man of subtle courage.

Belief in Correspondences

I don't go around with the belief in correspondences circling in my head as I turn any corner in Paris, or San Francisco, or Portland, & I doubt Baudelaire carried on that way, although the method for poets who walk, the Whitmans, the Olsons, well, we're out there for a reason, & it's not the shortest distance between two points, but labyrinthine meandering, looking up down & around for nothing in particular. Today out of peripheral vision I saw a tree stroll down the street. New spring shadows of limbs across asphalt. At the far end of Pleasant, (sure, I could long for Boulevard Saint-Germain or Telegraph Hill, but don't), I saw a mirage of a man smoking, but no cigarette smell, & just after I greeted one of his cats, "Hello, Gato!" the train running parallel to Forest Avenue pulled a black tank car reading GATX before the blue Boston & Maine boxcar. I saw a goddess cleaning out the last empty bottles under the seat of her car dressed in the tightest of blue jeans outside the Redemption Center. After the clerk at the wine store loaded up my linen tote bag from Polaine on rue du Cerche-Midi, the streets on the way home lost all familiarity presenting strangers at every corner who wanted to talk, carry on, be surprised, until at the crossroads of home & imagination the last of a snow bank pulled back to reveal the coldest of rhinestone hearts long off its invisible gold chain sparkling in the sun like real tears of love abandoned in anguish.

Two Sides of a Mood

I got down. My mood. I don't often. I wept, inside. It lasted over an hour. I drove through darkness like impinging walls in broad daylight, or a forest at night. On the other side there were no words, but invisible signs like those preceding the intention of making a mark drawn by Tapies, or a shape composed by Smithson, say, the *Spiral Jetty*, upon which a man could walk as much to the center of the earth as the center of himself, but without yet moving a stone, a pure sign in the middle of the bodily sculpted mind, beforehand. All of a sudden other voices chimed in like the aftermath of the dream-sign <Chorus Women Lament> she said, "Love," then another sung, "Life is Art!" I was on the street by that time, when a beautiful Asian woman stepped out of a storefront on the arm of a blind man. Her columnar skirt, her narrowest pointed shoes, each of which I turned away from refusing anything more than that briefest glance, in his honor. Then, listen to this, I couldn't make it up, the most regal of young African girls walked a walk you rarely see on this continent, glided, the African girl, whose nameplate I would have read, if I could have caught up, but she flew up Middle & then Exchange, making the most of her break from housekeeping down at the Regency Hotel, restoring my mood to the coolest hue, say an indigo blue brushed by the impossible.

Where to Next?

Salem, Barcelona, Seattle, Providence, Raleigh, Kilkenny, Galway, Tampa, Napa, Denver, Durango, Mazatlan, Malta, Portland, Scarborough, Plymouth, Bristol, Halifax, Aix, Avignon, Zagreb? I quickly think of Rimbaud making it alone through the snow to Stuttgart. D. H. Lawrence with his wife recording his travel across the mountains of Sardinia. Basho wandering out of Tokyo toward Kyoto, talking to friend & disciple, Sora, both jotting things down. My old friend, Robert Hellman, heading out of Copenhagen for the last time on the ferry, possibly singing deeply under his breath, just as I used to hear him in Gloucester, Mahler's, *Songs of the Wayfarer*.

The Goya Express

When I went to Spain I rode the *cornada*, gore of the bull. A wound as long & deep as the first cry of birth reaching the outskirts of the last whimper of old age. At every stop along the way, in every village, at center of great cities, my Soul bowed down before the black blood & hair, eyes, pants & shoes, the secret air above all the women giving directions.

Going a Bit Out of My Way

for **George Duggan**

Since he asked about the work I made a concerted effort, going a bit out of my way, later in the day, to drop it off. Generosity often pays off in strange ways. After I spent a few minutes pointing out pieces that may be of interest to a man whose taste doesn't gravitate to anything overly literary, choosing things drawn from daily life instead of an esoteric tradition. I got back in the car & drove off. By this time I would have been home, reading or cooking, certainly without the radio on, when the classical station promised poems of Baudelaire put to music by Debussy, again, diverting in yet another different direction to hear all five. Now, as much as I was intrigued to know the choices made by one of my favorite composers from the work of a writer I adore, as much hearing the tone to which the theme of lost idyllic Time rescued in sad recollection reached by the voice of the tenor, as much as I felt my own life enhanced driving down Route 3A in Marshfield, Massachusetts with two giants of Art & Poetry & Music, I preferred to read the work alone at home accompanied by the words' own thunderous, subtle, magnificent silence.

Rose Up, Reaching Down

Where this dream came from I'm not exactly sure, although earlier in the evening stunned to hear Paul Robeson sing the flowing, guttural, "Scandalize My Name." In fact, it was well documented, the tape on a flawless machine winding around & singing out to me & my little *banderilleros*, (actually I knew they were children of migrant workers) or angels, who couldn't keep their hands off the spooling mechanism as it went round, but when I tried to keep their hands off, they showed me who was boss with supernatural strength in hands, my little grape pickers. Produced by the Chilean State Opera, the *Folk Gospels of Chile* rose out through a single male voice in loving Spanish tongue accompanied by a lone guitar, superb guitar, subtle, sophisticated, peasant, at the same time, reaching down to the primitive under the jungle underwater sounds like that of the two-string *rutilio* plucked with a thin stone used as pic I once heard played by an overseer on a plantation just outside Veracruz.

Reverencing

Frayed-wire mornings after night's clarity depicts oppositional frameworks: knowledge, power, & hubris versus discovery, creativity, & humility, the latter the arsenal of the poet. Especially after the intervening hinge of the dream expresses the word *reverencing* in place of the word *referencing*, reinforcing the phalanx of his method.

They Exited upon a Stage

Lifting my head from dutiful attention, Time had dissolved into a concentrated tincture, metallic in sheen, & sharp across the cold harbor, horizon line, & sky. Another day had practically come & gone, night coming on. Look, right now, the square window of the top floor of a building has caught the round sun in it sights. In back of me her silence has a resonant beauty. Last night I dreamt of a museum show of Greek art. A large round stone curators called a *Solstice Stone* had a hole in the middle, painted gold with edges resembling waves or sunrays, which would cast a shadow on the ground or wall, when penetrated at solstice. As the curators were leaving, they exited upon a stage, curtain billowing, while I followed them as ancient priest & priestesses, wondering how I could learn the secrets of their egress.

April Fool

Rarely disappointed to see the last of March pass on, only to have trepidation at traditional warnings against optimism indelibly marked like tattoos on April first. Thirty-two minutes to midnight. Made some inquiries, outreaches, filled out forms & questionnaires. Let's face it, the system has little use for real live poets. I'm not sure exactly how they're arranged right now, but the lower floor of the Prado once held Goya's *Saturn* at one end, flanked in between by *The Sabbat*. Carried both images around with their accompanying text for three days in my black canvas bag as a talisman, along with voluminous copies of my résumé, which as I mentioned to one interesting stranger I handed it to, is not really me.

In the Words of Amiri Baraka at Mass College of Art

It was good to catch up with someone from the literary lineage. Friend of O'Hara & Olson, Amiri Baraka has always meant business, & last night when he blasted Auden for his quip, "Poetry doesn't do anything," showed what poetry can do, accusing one tenth of one percent of people running everything in this country, acknowledging our backward president as one of those corporate killers, ne'er-do-wells in youth spreading their seed all round rising to positions of oppression, the audience could all feel it, this rant against all those who feel a moral obligation to be against other peoples' pleasure, the culture or absence of it most think comes from TV, inventing the *lowku* opposing it to the Japanese haiku, knowing most of the world is not white & that the direction of the world will be decided by them, which is news to someone, I guess, laughing, that blowing whitey to hell may not be such a bad idea, but hey, he's here too, with some of his own people, reminding us that it was not by choice, but by terror, the slave ship pictured in his play I wrote a bad paper on in senior year in college when he was still known as Jones, just to throw all that incendiary language of his in the face of yet another incompetent teacher I despised, Baraka calling for the young students in the audience to, "Read read read! You may never get a chance again, you women gonna get pregnant, you guys jobs for the mon, & come home exhausted fall on the bed asleep, what you think you gonna read Aristotle? Publish yourself, go to Kinko's, make a Kinko's book out of what you believe, distribute them around yourselves. Be creative! What you going to produce other than expensive feces? Study now!" Then a grand poem about his grandmother where he conjectures that if the people of his race can figure out why their grandmothers were always humming, he hums it, sings it, raps it, drums it, & plumbs the answer, as if it were the Aum of the sound of the Universe, the hum goes on as a kind of preverbal *choric* chant like the Gregorian records he ordered as a librarian in Puerto Rico in the service because he & the other servicemen didn't know what they were, but wanted to, along with the twenty volumes of Kafka because they didn't know him, but wanted to, & the grandmothers hum as antennae as radar for what they knows comes eventually inevitably as trouble & the devil the rent bill & the man & Baraka lifts that tone up to around some pitch he learned from Miles or Coltrane when he mused on liner notes for the latter's album in 1964, **Live at Birdland**, *One of the most baffling things about America is that despite its essentially vile profile, so much beauty continues to exist here*, tearing that tone up out of the crib where rats threaten at night filled with anguish a pain inherited before birth we whites don't ever *get* lifting it way up past stars past death that realm of infinity where horses of the apocalypse are colorless.

"Slaves weren't Allowed No Drums, So They Made the Banjo"

With the whole world out there waiting. With the whole world out there waiting for contact, I stay here a few moments with the lone sunflower she picked up at the farmers' market days ago to greet me when I came home from work, stem sturdy as an ivory peg leg, gummy *ichor* secreted from stamens, petals gentle as her parting whisper this morning, also keeping me company now. "A whole field of sunflowers," the market girl said once, "out of which you can see nothing else." Making this sunflower, by comparison, lonely, but strong. Which road today? Up brick-walk State, down Spring to Pleasant. Sounds easy, doesn't it? As if a music could play in the head instead of words. I'll try that out there. Purely instrumental: free time spent plucking strings against the goat-gut head of a banjo between synapses.

Goya Records his Fascination

Why Araby? Why the carnivalesque? Somewhat grounded, haunted by the primal. Suddenly an American black man lands on the pages of the **Bordeaux Album**, where Goya records his fascination with the snake-handler at the fair. Dressed in a sort of colonial garb, the performer balances the heavy load on top of his head. On that night the sky was an arabesque of serpent belly. Yet, freer, there in France, than in similar lengths of chains back in the States, in 1828.

Perhaps Some Were Decoys

Plenty of rich folks wants to fight.
Give them the guns.
–Woody Guthrie

Knew it would eventually plummet. The gunshot I hear exiting the L.L Bean factory for lunch, co-workers out there on the walkway into & out of the building sitting in Adirondack chairs eating sandwiches in a trance, staring beyond a meager stand of trees separating them from the firing range. I was on the water in the dream canoe last night, when the rifle shot shot within earshot. I looked up & saw the stand of trees acting more dense, a serious camouflage for the invisible shooter. I tried to peer in simply to find out if I were a target. Single shot, but mimicked the ones from lunch. After a few seconds I picked my head back up & looked around. There were more canoes on the river, & a bunch of ducks placed strategically near them. Perhaps some were decoys. For five weeks now I've been trying to figure out the nature of the power behind this company. On Friday one of the marketing types breezed through with one of his paper mock-ups in hand checking out, & trying to impress the youngest group of factory girls. They'd have none of it. In the dream I voiced my astonishment about anyone's difficulty shooting sitting ducks. The marketing guy's picture is up on a wall along with about twenty of the rest of his ilk on a bulletin board in an air-conditioned corridor. Not one picture, however, of anyone from the sweltering quarter-mile sewing floor.

Begin Practicing

Physically exhausted after a long work week in which machines crank up before the allotted six o'clock hour, or else. Yet, exhilarated to let the language speak for itself, its color, the blueberry ocean. Buddy came by to fix my own, shattered parts all over the place, saying his daughter, a twelve-year-old "pre-adolescent," as she refers to herself, also likes to write stories. What I like about these blue-collar guys is lack of pretension, no calculated maneuvering. Go to any writers' conference, & that's practically all you see, the dodges & feigning, testing, power-mongering, preening. Here, everything is clean & clear. It's physical, leaning toward courage over pride. I told him the best advice he could give the child was to practice heightening each of her senses, & see what language results from the method. He was going camping this weekend with the whole family in the new pop-up vehicle, & you could see in his eyes, the added brightness at that moment, that he couldn't wait to share the message with her, & begin practicing on the mountains, trees, wind, wildflowers, all along the dirt paths, himself.

Right on Time

Off to work, what else? That's my class, after all. One side grandfather bolting the old country to run a small grocery across from mostly Irish St. James Church, but then gave so much away during the Depression ended managing meat for IGA. The other, born here, ancestors robbed of "Fitz" at Ellis, sold tea & coffee from a horse-drawn wagon, & supplemented Depression hard times in vaudeville stage shows with three musical sons. Blue-collar immigrants, if you view things from this side. But from the other over there they began as honest, industrious farmers in Mayo, & scholars in Kilkenny. All I'm leading up to here in as spontaneous fashion as I've garnered from America, & take as impetus from their blood energy is that on the way to work full white moon was going down over my left shoulder just like that evening on the other side of my life, when young, at twenty, just outside of Split in the then Yugoslavia, only moon rising & sun setting, then, today moon seen over left shoulder, sun slowly dripping wet above the Calendar Islands in Casco Bay, I pulled into the driveway at work right on Time.

Why We Want to Go Live with Wild Animals

Good reasons why we want to, every now & again, go live with wild animals. Civilization's taming taken too far, false talk, minor & major betrayals, lack of rule of instinct, cologne, white bread, SUV carbon monoxide, & the Oval Office. When we walked Back Cove on Sunday in order to beat the torrential downpour that inevitably fell that afternoon, she spotted the Black-crowned Night Heron hunched over hugging the estuary inlet in spite of all the foot traffic, & invisible to everyone but her keen eye, as if they recognized one another. Its one-legged balancing act touched her peripatetic core, a migration of two kindred Souls. Just yesterday the overnight security guard told me that the bobcat across the way emerged before dawn led by the red eyes of her new kitten glowing in the dark meowing its sweet entreaties to him. I could see, just for a second or two in his own eyes, a desire to go off with them, instead of gathering up his things, & as he said, not reading the paper when he got home, but watching tv until his wife went off to work.

Verging on Ecstasy, on Intimacy, on Raucousness, on Love

This time around a calendar square without bounds for September first emerged as a vortex for the rendezvous of purely feminine light limned in new shadow with an active, pollen-filled, dusty, almost out-of-control masculine wind, where up here in northern reaches the combination produced hours verging on ecstasy, on intimacy, on a gentle, audible raucousness for two people with heightened senses in tune with a myriad of trees & the demarcations of city streets at the same time, exchanging random language on the entire phenomenon, on Love.

Goya's Sturdy Knifegrinder

Walked in Seville today, past the cathedral where Goya's *Justa & Rufina* stand straight on the sacristy wall. When I left I was still looking up. A red-tail hawk stood broad-winged, opaque, in endless, open air. Further on I bumped into the local fishmonger, whose tools were worked on by an ancestor of Goya's sturdy *Knifegrinder*, now in Budapest. Marked the spot on my square map of a round world, which is turning like a grindstone, on which I try to sharpen my boundless senses as often as I can.

Cross of Eternity

Should have recorded this at the time, but making a living takes a lot these days. Blue of the jay circled toward the black of the wrought-iron fence at the same time as the reddest red of the cardinal curved away from the Norwegian spruce, leaving the blur of the cross of eternity, which could never occur again, while lightning later in the day etched it into history, the page of which is filled in in the quiet hour, between three & four in the morning by a workman's hands near exhaustion.

Mythic Tale

From my experience it's not when you're down & out, necessarily, & I know a lot about that, it's more when you're liable to be on the verge of success that they'll jettison your name face serial number. Watch out. You're loveable losing. Make some strides, win a prize, write something wondrous, or worse, of worth, & hell, the social landscape gets denuded. If you're lucky, one friend by the end, said Thoreau, who must have known as much about that as he did a bean row, or the Micmac mythic tale that moose was whale once.

Beauty & the Beast Dream

The natural propensity of language at that time of the morning, crossing the bridge between sleep & wakefulness, toward metaphor. However, I simply told her that in wanting to compare her body to something there was nothing to compare it with, whereupon she told me of her own "Beauty & the Beast Dream."

"There was a large man with balding red hair & a back filled with tattoos, who wanted to impress a young girl he loved by hunting down & offering her 300 oysters, but the father would have none of it, so the old sailor simply went over & sat with the young girl on a bench, where they were so happy next to the bag of the possibility of 300 pearls."

Up for Air

I must be some kind of sea creature to open a $1 can of jack mackerel with its four gutted frames, scraping fins off, removing major bones, mixing in celery & seaweed for a sandwich. Of seal or sea-lion family, perhaps, which if I come up for air at the wrong hole in the ice some polar bear could turn me into a toy for its own amusement, or an Eskimo divvying up my liver with fellow hunters while still warm.

Past Discarded Nets

Past discarded nets, nylon blue, pink, mostly green, down to two guys mending a large one made out of sturdier material, down to the X-Ray Gear Berth & Yard Marsden Hartley would have loved, what with the scene right out of his Nova Scotia sojourn: eleven men lined up along wharf's edge, five sitting, six standing, all casting or jigging for that still handsome mackerel. Between the *Sara Kathryn*, the *Melissa Sue* out of Fairhaven, *Rachel T* out of Cundy's Harbor, the *Cheryl K* based here in Portland, or even little *Kimberly J* from Cape Elizabeth, it's a lost man's world, long gone, dream world, or as it is anywhere where Woman is nowhere to be seen, desolate, abject netherworld.

Goya's Dog Today

I saw Goya's dog today. It offered the answer why the artist kept all but its sad, hesitant head hidden behind a wall. According to the curators Goya painted these "Black Paintings" fast, getting the gist down, ignoring minor details. This black dog on the main street today, the one on a leash led by a man more smoke than flesh, well, mange of neglect seeping through the coat would have been better served by a mortared wall than my averted gaze through dark sunglasses.

For a Few Passing Moments

Up at four. That's my rhythm. Staccato of three quick words, turning the ignition. Get out under the dark sky. All red lights blinking for the benefit of those working for the man, who may see stars, but not this early, & may see the harvest moon, but not as burnt-meadow orange as we did last night from our proletarian porch, binoculars checking out deep craters pocking moon's surface with less burnished sunlight. I carry weary, entropic bones away from work, where the smell of lentils on the stove is a delicious welcome home. A beer, & two ladles of soup. Read a few messages, shower. Then through dense fog I see a huge tanker heading out of port. Why tankers give so much joy is beyond me. The first thing I wonder is whether I can catch its name on the stern, knowing full-well no tanker can compare to last night's harvest moon. But it's the *Moondance* from Valletta. Life can be like that sometimes. Dreams come true. I've always wanted to go to Malta, probably because of Keats, given that he managed to take the journey during such a quick lifetime. (Way things are going, pretty much given up on *that* idea.) Today, however, for a few passing moments craggy hills, the brutal blue heat, & a gentle voice, centuries old, echoing off fortress walls from Valletta, Malta came all the way here to me.

Eddie Vega

One could pretty much tell which school he'd graduated from as he turned the corner of the wharf, surprised to see us, demurring, asking if he should find another place to fish, but of course not I replied he was as free as we were: Eddie Vega, hard knocks. With his dark glasses & bandana I thought at first he was Asian, especially when he mentioned he was from Lowell, although really from Trenton, a place I told him I couldn't wait to get out of whenever I found myself there, as if he needed that reminder. Sent back early by his father to Puerto Rico. Got out of the ghetto, he said, the hard way, as I already pointed out, first back to Trenton at 13 & a half with his shoeshine box & a knife bigger than he was. Boxer. No one to tangle with, a fly-weight most likely who volunteers his time at two clubs in Portland, but doesn't go for their European style of fisticuffs, his is African. When I mentioned Ali he perked up contradicting my idea of dance with his own of flying around the ring not getting hit, winning the Golden Gloves in Jersey, almost went to the Olympics. A handsome kid in that way of the trauma trailing the man, forty-one to be exact, he pulled up his shorts to show what he called his chicken legs, which weren't that passed the knees where the thighs bulged. Learned his style, though, from a Hungarian, his parole officer, who when I asked his name, Eddie became reluctant to try to spell it, honoring the man, he said, as a father figure, who put him & kept him on the right track, but there it is: Z-a-h-e-d-i.

Sadui

He chased us all the way down St. Germain Street in Boston just to return a book I'd left on the table at the restaurant. Granted, it was Yeats's birthday, & two days away from Kathleen's, & a week before the solstice, when the nights preceding it never really darken, but Sadui didn't *have* to go so far out of his way, running the two blocks after us, although I'd complimented him on his good looks when he brought the wine, thinking he must have come from a long line of Thai kings, born in Bangkok, he told us. I mentioned to the female owner, with whom I'm friendly, where we were staying, but I was still puzzled just how Sadui tracked us down, long out of sight of the place as we were. Perhaps he simply followed the instincts & lead of the book in hand, Czeslaw Milosz's **Road-side Dog**!

Goat & Camel

We'd had lunch already, but I wanted to see what goat meat looked like, so we stopped in next door to the Somali place on St. John Street, where the old butcher obliged. It's bright red, & sinewy. I asked how he cooked it, so he brought us behind the partition where there was a restaurant you'd never guess existed from the outside, like an African secret, no awning or façade. He talked Abdellah into giving us a scoop of meat & rice, for free. To taste, for free. Free to taste. It was anti-American, that's for sure. The music pleasing, & the television entertaining men at three tables. We sat down with our cache, my woman explaining her vegetarian ways, but willingness to try the rice, which she complimented as tribal faces beamed back. I stuck a *finnif* in his hand early on, so he brought some tea, & explained, in answer to my wife's question about the sign "Camel" outside, that no, here they have only goat, but back home, if a woman gets married, the dowry is paid in goat *or* camel. Delightfully anti-American, & downright exotic for an afternoon, snow in the offing, & most everyone else heading to the mall.

Mouth of Time

We went too far, which for me is always just far enough, past Vessel Services, past where I saw the wharf rat & osprey & seal pair, down to the unknown, unnamed pier, where a boat I didn't even take eponymous note of unloaded bucket after bucket of fish. It was anachronistic. Here, through the normal series of winches they'd drop the load upon a conveyer tray, where as fast as the hand of man inherited from generations of handling this species, back to Cro-Magnon, at least, they picked the best, dumped the rest. Right there on the dock, through a big hole: trash fish from the by-catch! If that's not a sin, I don't know what is, what with the three Asians, two youths, one middle-aged woman, & two older white guys, diagonally, in full-view of the waste, casting humble rods out into grey-scum-topped water for a single mackerel, blue, or striper. Hundreds fish lost to the anonymity of Eternity to just one pulled up to the mouth of Time.

On Marginal Way

Poets & mapmakers, so much in common, compass Souls at sternum & solar plexus. Bloom's shoes tracing Joyce's footprints in Dublin all the way from Paris & Zurich. Today, after reading the latest atrocities on women gathering firewood at the outskirts of camps in Darfur, suddenly, anachronistically in my path, another refugee from Sudan, (what with Maine sheltering the largest of that diaspora), paused in colorful robes, possibly confused by the sudden snow squall, quickly renegotiating her bearings on Marginal Way, of all places, in Portland. Snug in my vehicle, I tried not to stare, tried not to turn to look too hard at regal gait & beauty surrounded by swirl of snow, but she caught me in her own sight staring back, seeming to forgive my wonder, curiosity, appreciation, perhaps recognizing something akin to old griot eyes in the village, going about recording local histories, that last a thousand years, remarking boundaries, mapping the consequential.

Exchanges in Languages, Glances, Mask, & Doll for Self-Revelation

I had a big smile going on, which brought out a certain amount of consternation from folks in the middle rows of the bus, while those in back were too far away to get distracted over that. Two African women in their hospital blues & name tags were riding the crest of happiness, gratitude for both the end of a seven to three shift & a chance to riff in rhythms their native language offered. The avian reaches of some of those high-pitched lilts, along with deep valleys of barely audible breath bore a meaning only music can carry, & of course, once they knew the smile was in response to this foreign tintinnabulation the solos extended, & even a bit of body language thrust out of exhausted bodies. When one got off I asked the one left alone where she was from, where her friend was from, & what language they were speaking: Congo, Rwanda, French & Swahili. After telling her how much I enjoyed eavesdropping on their conversation I mentioned the mask from Congo we got in Paris. Just then the young girl who'd moved her bag to make room for me said to be careful of the mask it might crack. Funny, she should say that, I told her, because that's just what happened on the plane trip home. She laughed her exaggerated laugh saying she never lets anyone touch her porcelain doll so it won't break, commenting on its beauty, her cheeks beaming ecstatically heavenward even more than the way her doll does, I'm sure. Asked how old the doll is, when it was made, she rolled her eyes, again, & came back down with 1998. By about that time my stop was coming up quick, & I recommended some music back across the way to the African citing *Tinariwen* as a group from Mali, you know, where the Dogon come from, but she didn't. Well, it's a big country I must have said, when she uttered, the lone word, "Continent," correcting my dumb intellectual slip, but forgiven by the others much faster than I forgave myself.

To the Hilt

Nothing comes easy, but I love difficulties, and difficulties love me.
-Robert Frank

It's not that one's an artist one day, regular guy the next. Direction of the energy, & intensity of it might change, turn raw, get jagged, but it's there despite nagging distractions, including the day job. Can get wearying, too, especially if you write something of worth, or paint something, the first getting published ten years later, which recently happened, or the painting never sells. Core belief might remain, white Paris cat staring from framed postcard, brother Theo, the reader or two or three, loving wife. If lucky! I didn't work all that hard today, mostly looked at photographs, someone *else's* work: saw a breast below a smiling face; a bull still standing with a sword to the hilt through its neck; cityscapes of light & dark; images juxtaposed in the developing tray; & Kerouac playing the typewriter. Robert Frank taught me the value of energy spent on a daily basis, those sort of moments toward longevity.

The Dark Embers

That's the way I thought it, too. Getting up today as if out of a crypt with broken bones, but not heart, joy at just being alive for another day, for anything that strikes me, the whole world striking all possible bearings drawn upon the wide & vertical universe. So a little photograph by Robert Frank, *Old Woman/Barcelona, 1952*, goes a long way to remind me how ludicrous it is to rank works of the best artists, just as the grove I passed along the road today leading into a tangled, unseen mystery beyond seemed equal to the minor cleft & meaning between last night's rising moon & Venus. The prized package of Chesterfield cigarettes the back of her left-hand touches as lightly as the camera captures the dark embers of her Soul.

At the Center of Art

It may well be at the center of all art. Its eventual, unspeakable mark. Certainly, courage is not conscious, learned, nor necessarily, given. Inherited? Perhaps, but blood is not always that quick, & something on the order of picador's thrust, *banderillero's* barb, or finally, matador's sword, offer evidence of scar & wound called courage. It's all unconscious, & beyond anyone's claim. After all, few can capture it: for example, the upraised right hand of the man before the firing squad in Goya's *The Third of May*, or Hemingway's purely visceral understanding that, "the bravery of the bull is the primal root of the whole Spanish bullfight."

The Handsome Face

Sunrise welded itself to the glass façade of one of the downtown buildings this morning at a new angle one week from fall, somehow reminding me of the gold watch I got from my grandfather, just before, or after his death. Well, it wasn't gold, & didn't take too long for it not to work at all. But I remember taking it out of the top drawer every once in a while, taking a good look at the handsome face, both hands telling me what Time it would never be again.

Triptych of Time

I

Almost lost them, the last sweet days of summer in September, when hours can be sweet & fully appreciated without regret, if lived as intensely as the same last hours before death, should one record them to a loved-one, say, or a notebook. Almost lost ability to write by hand, keyboard magnetically, gravitationally drawing fingers down, but black pens on yellow legal pads stand at the ready attempting to gather days' events in the net of memory. Why do I want to say "Future Memory?" Is this act of capturing something absent, memories that haven't come yet, this act of seizing in the absoluteness of now, (that acrobatic tightrope), stealthy hunt for language, which is life, not inclusive of the Future?

II

Waning crescent moon rose earlier in the week just before the sun, slender as a mathematical sign. Then, next morning disappeared into the invisibility of the new. Affectionate words, what were they? Flesh seems timeless on her. Never lose sight of the body in the context of language, & you will never lose sight of language. My friend & I stood before the Matisse fairly dumbfounded at his ability to throw so many colors past internal censors of objection & critique. In *The Three-O'clock Sitting* the model stands in the middle of the room without being the center of the painting. Turquoise & white abstract stripes are centered, & our eyes circle round the room in joy. Look out the window at infinity. Model draped in towel, frontally, shown naked in the mirror from behind at an angle against all laws of perspective. Little dab of brown paint purring on the floor puns heated sexual aspects of harmony in the piece without the slightest hint of vulgarity.

III

Worked. Prepared squash soup. Watched politics of an outmoded system, & made plans to join protest in DC. Saw hawk, gull, mass of sparrows. Twin bulrush, flowering mullein, New England asters. Walked on sand & asphalt. Took sun on water in. Concentrated as hard as prayer: asking forgiveness, & handing it over. Noise, which even toward the end we might hesitate to let go of became part of life. Huge oil tanker, *African Future*, with blue hull & orange deck sailed past at 12:50 PM, September 3rd, perhaps instigating the idea of an all-encompassing circle with invisible boundaries, essential to transgress, contents showing the wealth of Zero. Wine, red. Food, raw & cooked. Touch supplementing words. Leaves remaining green. Time, mind (body), language changed.

The Aesthetics of the Fragment

I go for that, I told them in an essay: the notebook, fragment, random jotting. Not without purpose, not just anything, but the result of desire & impetus. Out here on the balcony with the dahlias having weathered wind, thunder, lightning, (they didn't flinch), drinking rain in all night overnight, both pots growing from toddlers to adolescents in half a day. Keeping me company in lieu of any mail today. As they weathered the storm I thought about the thesis, *the aesthetics of the fragment*. It has a lot to do with our innate refusal to see any object in some way other than inherently whole, at the same time cultivating a fondness for that which is missing, that which is consubstantial to the ruin.

Marble Stele of Kosmetes Sosistratos

I carried it around, no heavy load, as if the wind itself were moving sculpture. Lifted it against post-mortem reports of the civilized world in the daily papers. The marble stele of kosmetes Sosistratos, which stood so long in the *Diogeneion*, the Gymnasium in Athens. I ran there once in a dream, calling it the Palace of Health. I can't read the inscription written across the chest of the abstract torso, nor that etched below the life-like genitals. The brilliant sculptor knew the dead no longer needed limbs once put to such good use on that good ground in that good life, but generously left the head, the sex, the words, intact.

Seventh Century Day

A whole pride of Assyrian lion clouds raced along the horizon, changing colors as the day went on: red, bronze, yellow, white, hungry for the sun.

Triptych of Time II

I

Called the wind *brutal*, when asked by someone going out the door to face it. Thought better of it soon after, *natural* more appropriate. The hawk with pigeon in one talon, hassled by crows, flew straight back at them, no cruelty involved. After the skirmish a jagged line of feathers stuck to driveway asphalt by some bloody substance at the quill. I can't say the same for man. Witness it, (brutal cruelty), in a glance; overhear it in mere tone of voice; find evidence left in daily records.

II

I would, I'd want, not want it all, want to write it all, from swirl of pigeons circling turret of Victorian across the road, windows & all, in limited rod & cone vision of small red eyes, to monstrous cloud carrying big snow squall I walked out to get surprised by, as nothing but a marine forecast could predict, enveloping like a sort of Christo wrap around all 365 Calendar Islands in Casco Bay, & dwarfing into miniature the black tanker, *Montiron* out of Monrovia, berthed for days unloading oil at the tank farm across the harbor. No squall fell at all, at least on land, but by the time the cloud covered the entire area, at exactly 1300 hours, the white white container ship, *Margit Gorthon* out of Helsingborg, cut right through grey air water cloud, at which time I felt close to Homer recording his Catalogue of Ships, when all I had to capture it, no one around to voice it to orally, was a trusty felt-tip pen, & the back margins of one of the few dollar bills left to my name.

III

I wouldn't want the sun to turn that corner before praising her, her light, which even in her absence remains a vibration, a heat driven into the walls, the sheets I'm long out of early in the morning. With her long gone to her own strenuous practice, I read writings on Cy Twombly out of a massive tome, a series of early criticism & later praise for his digging under the symbol to the sign, & below the sign to the signifier, past that to the indecipherable mark holding on to its own mysterious meaning. All this in the sun yet to turn the corner away from her absence, which always earmarks a presence located in anticipation of her return, scratched out here in the exquisite void of the present, a roundness encompassing invisible, visceral edges.

Rembrandt's, The Rat-Catcher

I'm fond of the rat-catcher. Now, the rat-catcher has a great deal of knowledge, knowledge of the sort, again, I'm quite fond of, the nonacademic. This man's experiential credentials are voluminous. Can you imagine the filthy corners, dark barns, dank cellars this guy & his dwarf assistant have traversed, the obstacles & trials, errors, missed opportunities, tried again? It's real life! He has the apparatus & potions to conquer the fiercest threats, & yet, too, he owns this gnawing, intuitive hunch (stored up there at the top of his shoulder, as well?) that there's some connection to his curative calling & the Plague entering so many doors ahead of him without the courtesy of knocking. Yet, in this etching he's not articulate enough to convince his customer, who can't be bothered with such a low life.

Philosopher in Meditation

Celestial fire tended by man in thought at window balanced by earthly fire tended by the woman at the fireplace opposite. The Golden Mean based on Fibonacci's medieval calculation, in which each number is the sum of the two preceding numbers, rises measured within the spiral staircase. In nature the first step is called the body whorl, rising ultimately toward the Galactic Spiral. The sunflower has 55 such steps. In fact, math & history diminish before the genius of Art. The sum of all knowledge? Random heap of Rembrandt's linseed-oil-stained rags.

Around the Edges of the Accusation

We duck in out of the ordinary into the local art college library, where browsing Rembrandt, Rubens, Van Eck, what thought strikes me other than that I want only (wantonly?) to open a book unread by another eye, unopened by other hands. On the new book shelf the huge **Fluxus Codex** pleases me no end, documenting everything like the oscillation of my everyday disarray reassembled into order, or my penchant to store pages of work in boxes, & my long-held desire to publish pages in boxes, say, **Portland Steamer Trunk, or the Portmanteau**. Wolfli goes woefully untouched, & while I admire his decorative use of script, I loathe his choice of *Kraft Cheese* imagery, until young girls he molested start surfacing naked like *putti* around the edges of the accusation of his sainthood. Finally, Cezanne comes to the rescue in conversation with his blunt, workman-like, mechanic's language, pulling no punches, talking of soil & sweat, & the recognition that no one in the century surpasses Courbet, the builder, mason, his crudeness, his plastering of paint, suddenly linking us all, Wolfli, & even Annajarga modeling the Fluxus *Top & Bottomless Bathingsuit*, Cezanne adamant that he's mad for Courbet's coarse nudes.

Dance of Time

Keep the day in front of me as a dancer would, moving in & against Time. Turning the lights off, another bursts through. Taking eyes off one thing, another comes into view. Can one sustain this intensity all day & night, a lifetime long? Breath & memory have rhythm accompanied by waves of sound & light swirling in order & chaos to make & unmask a world.

Saving the Art of Dance

One of those dreams that proves the efficacy of a habit of keeping pen & paper by the bed, because by morning it was gone. Probably stemmed from a chance meeting with Lee Bellavance on Exchange Street the day before, when admitting the level of my ambition seemed questionable. Halfway through a race, still in contention. Race officials wondered how this was possible, given my condition, one of them referring to a propensity to gain weight quickly. Suddenly they altered the course. The track turned into shallow water. Waded in, then dove, seeking deeper channels. Declared the winner, to the shock of all involved. They gave me a two-year extension on my license to compete with a stamp of approval similar to the Chinese character for *man standing by his word*. A delayed addendum announced that I'd saved the art of dance by citing an ancient author, (whose footnote, including his name with the internal vowels of "a" & "e," disappearing under the erasure of the screen of the magic writing pad,) & that intercourse was good for participants while training, ultimately enhancing the nature & understanding of their performances.

Black Spanish Wine

Late at night, after black Spanish wine, in dreams, the dancer dances by herself. Alone, without me. I watch with pleasure her free & unencumbered movements, nodding smile, & knowing glances tossed my way. Driven by Lorcan *duende*, & Goyesque intensity, she's ravishing! As if Time's impact on the body were made null & void by Art.

Quick Step

Jot it down quickly, as if the sun itself sped up to leave, light continues to linger on the walls in mourning. Her flesh next to me brings Time down to its knees, while the dancer of the dream of the night before continues to resonate joyously in the wind of the open window, tramping in the dust of the open-air stage: the goat-legged girl.

Time, & Time Past

for **Paul Cronin**

Told her before leaving the house that I still carried the image of the full moon balancing on the horizon two nights before, practically stationary on the water despite earth's constant motion. So when Paul Cronin called me away from my desk a short while later, I wasn't surprised to hear him wax aesthetically about his own experience of it. Closer to it, after all, out there on the Eastern Prom, walking the dog, referring to the celestial body as "on fire," & almost mistaking it for sunset. It was joyous. Here was someone even more appreciative of the event than we were: best moonrise in all of his seventy-one years! Told him I told her I was still carrying it around myself, which made him pleased to think there may be words added to describe the phenomenon, acknowledging at the same time, nothing could do it justice. Mentioned how we looked through binoculars to see the ring of its periphery shimmering in a less than perfect circle, distorted by craters, or mountains, or merely distance. On the way home, at the intersection of Center & Pleasant, when a girl turned the corner, then another & another, it became apparent that a gang of international schoolgirls, five in all, sharing one ice-cream, was attempting to distract from the task of the narrative at hand. Yet, somehow they fit right in. Feminine beauty cannot be dismissed when attempting to depict the greatest moonrise in three-quarters of a century. Just before pulling into the garage, I made a point of avoiding the woman from Pakistan pushing her grocery carriage filled with empties. I've seen her up close, both times offering a *finnif* to lessen her toil. Ritual tattoos of three spiritual eyes in the center of her forehead are as ancient as the Buddha. However, she's in here only because at the last moment, one of the wheels fell from her cart, & lay there in traffic waiting for her to retrieve it. Time encompasses the memory of that beautiful moonrise. Time Past is integral to the wheel left flat on the street. Neither of which I'm willing to let go of today.

Older than Time

On Memorial Day we traipsed through Evergreen Cemetery seeing everyone, knowing none. Willamain, how wonderful an abandoned name. There was the widow of Captain Hopkins, himself buried at sea. Then we trekked back into town ourselves just to get out on the water. Missing the Peaks Island ferry by five minutes, we hopped on the *Aucocisco III* headed for Little Diamond, Great Diamond, & Long. Only in America will they restrict passengers from the top deck, I mean this is pure transportation, matey, keep pleasure out of it! You're right if you realize that Americans fear pleasure, love violence & control. We got off at Great Diamond, the other passengers, a number from the Caribbean, wished they'd followed suit. All alone on Great Diamond, Time on our side, Time inside, Time straight up, Time friend, Time together, sea's Time, sky's Time. By the Time the boat returned a bevy of people on the boat wanted the island, the island people the boat! Along the beach there I found a number of stones older than Time.

Secret Snow & Fish Bones

Snow fell in secret overnight. That's visual music, those five words. Then I swept it off the sidewalk & her car, seeing in the act staff & clef of a musical score. Earlier, at supper with her, I lifted a series of fish ribs still connected to its spine out of the soup I'd concocted over the weekend, seeing something in them quite similar to the pleasure offered by the visual music of secret snow.

This Thorn Tree

My friends, the blank page, & steady snow Bill says reminds him of his years in Switzerland, the 1638 farmhouse, pear kirsch the landlord made, that he & his wife, Pat, added to tea in white afternoons. The *Erviken* headed back out to sea just as the snow came in erasing its name on black hull. Another friend, the ink-scratched page, something akin to this thorn tree thrust up through the entire snowfall without piercing a single flake.

The View

We got out there early. The pearl of sun peeking through both shell lids: clouds & the top of an island stand of pines, irresistible. On the walk we saw New England asters, bayberry, bittersweet, bulrushes, crimson berries I can't name, but which spell out loud from every stem P-O-I-S-O-N, & then even a wild apple tree with fruit left at the top quarter just out of reach of other peripatetic Souls like us. She said she loves the deep colors of late summer classifying the season correctly, not fooled that it might be fall already. A boundary stone signaled us quietly, don't stop, go on, together. Near home, at the top of State Street right in front of Mercy Hospital, just when the world started to distract me back to its distortions, impingements, & constant trouble, she steered my gaze back down to the end of the street, where past the International Ferry Terminal, the same sun that invited us out in the first place, having conquered the day's clouds, shimmered off rippling water like a grace, a paradise, a transmogrifying philosophy of Nature.

Of a Stillness

Of a stillness. I found that. The nearest sound a thousand miles away. In a plane. In a recollection. A remembered murmur. Of a stillness. I found that. Inside. White birch bark hides glacial majesty & depth. The pain that drives one to one's self, ultimately welcome. No shadow of a bird ever spoke. Of a stillness. Roots of spring. Nothing. Nostalgic, nor romantic. Eye contact with her this morning resonating now. Of a stillness. Not prolonged, dogs start, hammers mark an end.

Collision with Eternity

One of those days unfolding without event, how'd Olson define it, that collision of one's own being with eternity? As much as I appreciate the clarity the sun now provides, higher in the sky, two-thirds of winter over, changing energies of nooks crannies gouges cracks indentations scars shadows of the largest boulders, they're subtly displayed, & discreetly read. I don't even mind responding to the woman who stops to say she envies me the day to myself, the trek the entire length of Oceanside. In fact, if I have expectations for such epiphanic experience, that minor intrusion erases them completely. I start to rethink what I said & should have, etc., the usual second guessing when one's driven out of the deep traveling well of solitude.

Then, suddenly, the falcon, which I spotted only once before perched on a sumac by the marshland makes a U-turn deciding to reverse its course toward the water (what's a falcon going to find there?) swinging at such low-level it's startling, gliding, both eyes beading right on mine as if trying to read my mind. It would have read pure exhilaration & joy, perhaps a wish to penetrate as deeply into those two eyes streaming directly at me, just behind the more pronounced raptorial beak, squinting, I swear, from the sun behind me. A good fifteen yards away it loses interest, takes a sharp right like a fighter jet, brandishing its silver underbelly, fluttering momentarily jagged wings, heading off looking for smaller, better things.

New Year

She talked of Time as continuous, practically eliminating Death. Whereas, he stopped it dead in its tracks, keeping the moment alive. Snow fell overnight without a single witness. Yet everyone heard it, internally, at the depths of their Soul. The phrase, *Keep an eye out for the music,* turned the whole world into song.

An Internal Chord

Watched the dark come on, landing on rooftops, the civility of apartment windows & streetlights emerging with it, accompanying it like some harmony, which could only be imagined, or painted, by a Whistler, say, as far away from Lowell as he could get, adding at the end some nocturnal title to the piece, intimating color could be heard. It's not that far-fetched. Last week at about the same turn toward dusk I saw a star & the crescent moon hang from separate branches of the same bare tree. What suddenly seemed a distant sound of infinity corresponded to an internal chord opening up in me.

Trouble with Time

That in itself would offer a brief insight into the matter: the trouble with Time spent on writing continuously separate from money. We were exhausted, perhaps even exhausting each other trying to figure out how to live, live, as poet & wife, both curses, which Creeley linked with death. Where to find a roof, four walls, & a few windows in this day & age, when one percent of the population owns most of this crude, architecturally crass, second-home-strewn culture? Not a lot to ask: an affordable rent where we don't have to fear rodents & rapists! But no, exhausted, & in bed early. Later, the moon hung in the sky for the second straight night, red & yellow, & clear at 11:43 calling on me to pay attention. I got up. Paid homage with attention. Binoculars revealed the lip of a giant crater jutting out at the bottom of the crescent catching light from the sun's rays, saying, "Risk & metamorphosis."

Time Guiding Her

The brutal absence. Everything here now has the immediacy of skin. The damned coffee pot, the lightning last night, some scrawled notes I took on her first day gone, where the phrase *sacralization with things of the earth* surfaced from the depths of a sermon haphazardly attended in order to get right with the world. Then a letter arrives with the imprint of starfish on stationery I bought for her, unable to think of anything else, kind of dumbfounded during the gift-giving holiday. July begins in two days, & again, I don't have anything to welcome her home. Focus on her so much, other things might get short shrift. So here, water pitcher, lord of balcony tomato plants; here, toaster, we rarely use; here, modern blinds, taken for granted; here, ceiling fan; right now you're all the skin, bones, visual & tactile flesh I can relate to. Hello fading light, receding Time, guiding her back, deductively, this way.

Reversal of Time

She saw me off to work filled with coffee & autumnal root soup looking as good as I could for the present gig, but unable to resist a complaint about the jacket, she cut loose threads off of at the edge of a sleeve. No stagnation. No reversal of Time. Rhododendron, a calliope in November wind. Bare trees drumming the surface of their landscape. Clouds, the sun & sea's children, playing tag & hide & seek. Bach had something like twenty kids. Joy & Beauty in color & words. If this were Franz Kline it would be three black strokes of thick brush resulting in thin lines of individual horse hairs abutting lacunae of primed canvas visible to a trained eye. Or Keith Jarrett, lengthy space held & prolonged between notes, piano foot pedals unafraid to add gritty percussive mechanics into the improvised score. Sun on water, now. Lone boat slowly against current, distant, reminiscent of Li Po rolling over Yangtze.

Hauling Sunrise Rim to Rim

From rim to rim, from beginning rim-arc rim all the way round, slowly, as slow as one wants life to be, when life is good, when life is good & slow, I saw it, limning, as if touching horizon, knowing full-well the bottom rim would show, exposing a small, expansive side & section of the universe to all privileged & alive who witnessed it. Taking a cue from Time's revolving illusion, apparent entropic ring, high C to gong, buoy bell to foghorn, steering my own direction down the street, wary & open to gargoyles' stare, pediments' plain enunciation, hauling former sunrise rim to rim, becoming constant presence, an internal illumination guiding me throughout the day, as if reading in that immediately-etched memory, a navigational chart, the way the grey-hulled oil tanker, *Acadian*, lumbered out of port just now, heading north, all the way to Saint John.

The Music of Time's Disappearance

Not much going on, but disappearance of day, time & light combining to wane goodbye. I keep my eye on that, too. Would have liked silence as background noise rather than builders banging, sawing, dropping, clawing money out of hours. They're long gone. Put on Bill Evans' *I Do It For Your Love* playing Paris in 1979, not so long ago, mere space between notes. Get up, touch her in passing on my way to the window to see what time clouds will tell. Fish-ribbed, "Just after six," they say. Moon appears half-full with the other half visible, but veiled. Car tail lights head home across the bridge expanse like red corpuscles snaking through my veins at pulse rates matching the music of Time's disappearance.

Cudgels Fell There

After revelers woke us up in the middle of the night, at the exactness of summer solstice, to put our arms around each other, two circles, two hearts, a few words, the afternoon found the sun standing at stasis above me, illuminating the text where the bull cornered by the ring squares the circle by killing. Off in the city I caught sight of both hands dangling at my side in the mirror of an elevator descending, reminding me of the carved shapes of cudgels Goya depicted two men using against the other, both descending into the heath they argued over. Yet, these two hands, (Rimbaud said he'd never own his), which could be seen by others as ugly, primitive weapons, descend there along with me in the mirror of the elevator as now sun seems to round the corner of the building where I sit outside silently as peacefully as far from involvement in any further violence as the gift of language can take a man.

Writing & Reading

Even immediacy of interruption, incorporating that into the present? Constant distractions at work away from the real work, reminding me that at this time last year I stood in front of the machine at 6:15 already sewing another bookbag for the backs of youngsters dreading the return to school. There, on the hot factory floor in front of the despotic machine preventing me from reading or writing, I'd sail to Venice where the *vaporetto* dropped me off with my stack of books & sense of absolute freedom on the little island completely covered in the mosaic of stone tiles surrounding a lone building, which I never entered, preferring to stretch out on the marble tiled *piazza* reading under the Adriatic sun in order to find my Soul in words. Distress at lack of freedom to read, that bondage, always led me to the margins. Look at me in Belgrade, content as hell even on the dollar-twenty-five a night barracks bed with a book, or roaming the streets in anxious freedom to stop & gaze in wonder. Coffee & walnuts this morning drove me to Mexico City, where we'd read in the forty-dollar a month boarding house living on pecans & red wine in luxurious joy. In Nice, my knapsack of clothes became veritably useless, showering only on the beach, sleeping out of doors for weeks. Freedom on the stones of the Mediterranean, reading. Fifty-two jobs: delivering brochures the entire length of Lynnfield Street at eight-years-old; teaching in fractured classrooms; factory worker in leather, fish, meat, & canvas; or underling in libraries, where they forbade my writing & reading. The margins I've carved out today. What will Lorca say? What pleasures, secrets, & insights could Duras, Cixous, Montale, Olson, & Dorn, offer my own Soul today? Blood shed on the page is there to be read.

At the End of Writing

When earlier I stayed up late to watch the fullest full moon at perigee rise dripping-wet out of the Atlantic, or stood counting lightning strikes as they approached until one struck the roof of the house two doors down, now I catch her entering the same ocean, gingerly, beyond waist-deep, & dunk, her little seasonal ritual she equates with renewal & ablution. Yet it's purely secular & sensual, & of course, sexual: just ask that gang of half-naked athletes prancing & galloping faster than the line of horses I saw across the channel, slowed down by saddles & riders. Open space, freedom, a sense of gratitude at her directing attention my way, & a bit of peace, almost tranquility, similar to the way Kerouac got to it after weeks of delirious struggle on the opposite side of this broad continent at the end of writing in Big Sur, just running out of words.

Poetry & Death

That fragment, the one with a secondary crack tracing subaltern rhythms, the one dropped between late-night meandering & sleep, made not of stone, nor ceramic, but language… the lone one having to do with brilliance in the realm of night… that clarity… fell into the sea. Held my breath, & dove. Resurfacing, she came out with the terrible story of witnessing the embalming of her sister by a stranger, which she tried to stop, believing her still alive. Sidled up close, & whispered, "Wrapped in a white shroud, my sister began to say two words only: *Poetry*…" The second word disappearing into the unfathomable depths of mourning in the dream.

Dirge

for **Guy**

White cat wondering. I know what you mean, I say, wordlessly back. Dirge in the air today. Silent dirge, overheard. A man who taught that life's too short to wrangle, now, smiles up from the urn, or down from where the air carries the Dirge like snow. The roof even with the apartment window turns into a long, long meadow, as if two men could have walked out there, never having met in person, their years of words like footpaths at the vanishing point, ultimately converging.

Oracular Time

Sun just up, tossing a deep-amber line of light across the harbor with the hissing sound of a spreading net. What would Sun fish for, but Souls? Before one note of traffic, a mourning dove chanted from a rooftop its three-note arc in a key equal to the cello. I admit it, I got caught up, resisting temptation toward more familiar desires, listening for previously unheard of answers.

The Death of Someone Close to Him

Got word late last night, where it borders on morning, of the death of someone close to him, when only hours earlier I'd recollected his about-face toward Spain. Add the coincidence of the bookstore calling to say both copies of Lorca I'd ordered, one for him, were in. Death's presence is essential in the ring; hovering around black sounds of *duende*; or ingrained on the terrible surface of blank page & canvas. This arid tear. Segovia arranging Bach. Goya etching graves.

Time, Truth & History

I prefer the Boston sketch, in which Goya's Truth stands naked, feet firmly on the ground, while Time, as usual, is in a big hurry, fast as the speed of light. History squat on a rock. Five times larger, the painting in Stockholm hasn't the life of the sketch. Truth dressed up in some organdy gown, while Time's grown older, & slower. History? Well, she's just an art student posing for some life-drawing class.

Goya's Hungry Time

Were we to judge the day by the sun, then this dark, infernal, this April rain accentuating the blackest, barest trees, may never really have begun. It may, instead, be the day Goya went deaf to the world. An unnamed day, filled with suffering dogs, & beautiful women bitten by Fury. Goya's hungry Time. The missing day taken out of the calendar in order to balance any minor Joy.

Why Jean Rhys Would Appear in a Dream?

Why Jean Rhys would appear in a dream is beyond me, but she wanted to talk on subjects ranging from wine to her sadness abroad while away from her West Indies home. She was gestural & aged, animated & deeply curious, as if desirous of adding to her unfinished autobiography. In fact, although my own recollection of the visit keeps it brief, her image remains intense, especially centered around her query regarding a specific "situation." I can only guess she meant writing. Whereupon we agreed, that in doing so one attempts to "master Time."

Death's Graffiti

Breaking through the mortal wall of Time, one hand holding a pen, where the brick of existence loosened, two eyes peering through, writing it down on the other side, the illegible scrawl.

I Saw Time

I woke up, looked out the open window, & saw Time. It hovered in the East, kindly, without intent. I heard it in the actions of men, & in the silence of distance. It balked at any linearity, but danced in Flux with a body made of ethereal energy, which included the past, & a bit of the next second. I saw Time, behind Death's mask.

II. Earlier Verse: *Stones Trees Names*

You know, verse
is a lovely thing.

It issues,
like vapors,

from the rock - **Charles Olson**

He who has kissed a leaf
need look no further. **- WCWilliams**

Name Painted on the Ceiling of the World

For the language
to be right, for it to contain
traces of valuable ore,
one has to exhibit patience, make sure
rhythm, first & foremost,
(internal spark leading toward combustion), erupts
from the cave, reverberates
out of the central core
of being, of breath.

Must practice rejecting, erasing
all false starts,
to start again.

Today,
tramping into nature for hours
I remained calm, steady, pleased with freedom,
but nothing struck me.
Suddenly the red-tailed hawk painting
the celestial ceiling tore
a memory straight out
of the bottom
of my soul.
A letter.

Ended up in the mailbox
of my first apartment. My address,
but not my name. I thought someone
was playing a joke: Rodney Birdsong.
I expected a crass inveiglement
Instead, upon opening it,
the beauty of the script blew my mind,
(it was 1969)
& the greeting, "Dear Son,"
made me realize
immediately
what I'd done,
but I continued.

Eventually, mother,
from the reservation, referred
to her son's Conscientious Objector status.
I stopped.
There must be a new tenant in the third apartment in the building
with only three apartments.
I went downstairs & knocked.
Yes, the kid my age,
Rodney Birdsong,
invited me in upon hearing
such profuse apologies.

The first Native American, first
conscientious objector, first person
from Oklahoma, most gentle
man from another race

I'd ever met,
forgiving my trespass ahead of time,
& educating me to the endless
possibilities of language
soaring at the center
of a stranger's
significance.

The Woman in the Paragraph

Protected by the elevated earth,
ferns whose habitat runs from Greenland
to Peru, seem like remnants
perpetual since the Devonian,
though in fact those seed-bearing
ferns became extinct, these are
appropriate for my cold-blooded
task this late September afternoon,
only to make my way toward a stone
of correct degree where the sun will
warm both sides of the amphibian in me.

II
The future air of Cuzco, I breathe it.
The dark columns of evening prone
on the furrows of this summering
hemispheric earth. Vegetal evidence,
separate from the city sweat of Lima,
cleansing; the beet soup my Polish wife
serves up in the forty dollar a month room,
where without red there would be no art.

Love Also Creates the Mask

Late, past the time of the first
crowd of friends
since youth,
at four in the night
the temptation
present
to step beyond, save
for the woman who learned
from three months' trekking in Nepal, contentment
need not reveal
itself
in a smile,
we might have gone
from freedom
to delirium,
in the ritual
before her
face, the words,
the dance,
began to…

Light of a Dark River

There is no grief
without cause of Love.

Night removes trees'
scrawled shadows

from buildings' ochre
walls, until vivid

moon begins again
to draw her own.

Winter lodges in March
bank to bank across the river,

calm snow resting there & on
the land before an onslaught

of sun & men.
Affirmations:

of earth redeemed, the dead
from Love are comforted.

Throw More Light

By 10:00 the light is nothing but heat, fire becomes speech & the end of August forces this pure space into memory. The iron-ore-eye of the lion, your grief, wakes upon the plain field of my desire. The heart enclosed in action, my life in your hands. Your flower within the flower within the flower within.

Rushes

These five hills
detrital abundance
southeastward,
are undiminished
by the burning
and final blackness
of their winter grasses.

Waters
they contain:
pond stream swamp
urge the gold of rushes
on the eye, ancient
flames at temperatures
nearing zero.

The Dying Leaf

> *He who has kissed a leaf*
> *need look no further.*
> **- WCWilliams**

Focusing
its tenuous hold
on the natural world, the desire to return,
Freud said, (Eros with dust
on his tongue) to inorganic matter, the leaf
captured by Man Ray
in an act of transformation,
substance to shadow.
A state no less vibrant
than before.
Calyx to Vortex!

Exotic Birds

Gold straw,
absorbed light of the field,
is now under me,
having put the hills
between me & a northwest wind,
alone all morning,
kept moving by a desire
for warmth, I settle
on this spot, a ridge even
with the tree line.

Male & female exotic
birds (for the chill of New England)
choose the top of a dead tree
to perform
an intricate mating ritual,
where amazed, I stay still & watch,
matched only by their patient
inherent fervor.

The Sturgeon River, or Merrimack

A confluence of desires,
these friends, rural
neighbors kept quiet
under the sudden
& heavy snow of November.
A thick Martha Washington bedspread
my father's aunt sent from the capital itself.
The grid of the field of cut
cornstalks just above
the snow, & the heads
of purple, red cabbage left row upon row, rendered
flowers by the season.

White, purple,
those Kerenyi called colors of Eleusis,
straddle the River,
which once fed
all of Cape Ann with sub-glacial debris
from the Merrimack Valley. Our talk, a theatre
of consequences: wood & food & pottery, carpentry & children,
painting & writing,
some of us to learn a method
for getting through
these imminent,
receding tomorrows.

From the Usual Gentleness

A collection
of haze
between the hills
not unlike the grey
underbelly of the hawk
yesterday. Making me
suspect I am not the first
out here, a rustling noise
differing from the usual gentleness
of the tall reeds' sway,
a kid breaks out, braking-
saying, if I have any matches.

I had wine in a honey jar,
an apple
in a napkin,
& a slice of bread,
homemade in the same bag,
but I was not prepared to share anything
except some Words,
Wisdom, thought wrenched out
of crisis. With no matches

he left, unable
to rise to the situation.

Kouretes

Sun darkened,
they strode up
Paleologos Street
in Peabody, Massachusetts,
the market's youngest boy
following
in procession,
the lamb's
hind legs
visible from the canvas
wrap slung over
his shoulder. The ritual
did not go unnoticed
between the row of sunflowers
now hungry out of the hot top,
& on the other side
the olive trees slouching heavily
from some blood or remnant
of that previous
time in them.

Circular Angle

for **Maria Luisa Katznelson**

Afternoon showing of the erotic
works of Pedro Coronel in Mexico City,
his white beasts & angels, stares of love
joining each separate limb, simple conjunctions,
permanent birthmarks on the not-long
dead. We were hot on the trail of simple lines.

Twenty-seven lines in *L'Age de Soleil,*
a print by Picasso given to a friend for his wedding,
the face of a boy like my intended son,
& the only thing I've missed since we left.

Before boarding the bus in the rain my wife & I shared our tarpaulin
with you. Once on the bus you didn't notice everyone moving
toward you, you were the soft reason,
sexual magnet.

I moved all the way back out of reach, where one other
pimply, nervous boy, a civil engineering student I thought
not to crowd to you, but eyeing me in a guessing
nervousness, I wondered what was wrong.

An empty space,
he sat next to me, opened a book I thought of equations & asexual
angles, but, well into the letters of **Young Werther**,

he was getting near the end, & it was you,
not me, who could have saved him.

Photographing the Dream

It's portable.
I've made it into a *retablo*.
Pitched out of the darkness of the dream,
she stands in sackcloth folds barely outlined against adobe.
So little wind in this New Mexican terrain, no sand visible
to the naked eye, but for a small silicate mound
hugging the threshold.
A washbasin juts out before her.
Where the mirror should have been: her own decision
not to look that way
again...

Georgia O'Keeffe, revenant?

I know the image marked my own change.
I bring it up now & again to ward off trouble
of my own or others' doing. She stays there,
sackcloth folds barely discernible from adobe.
(What are the waters of that font,
but holy?) It's portable.
I've made it into a *retablo*.

The level of the land ushers light in
at the edges of the vestibule.

Seemingly late,
by seeming.

Hearth

Out of this domesticity two gods manifest.
The girls walk to the child-care center along
the Serpent Merrimack, winding
past orchard hills & vineyards. A gut
connection uninterrupted at their leaving.
Time led by fingers prepares for the feast
of light, enter the evening sky, John,
naked after a full day's work.

Big-Tree Night

I wanted no more of the moon
revealed
than what you pointed out: apple sliver,
(the one our friend Bill called since childhood, "Turkish"),
which you pulled down to taste from the big-tree night
distance is.

Let it be the first
of night-time balancings: I recall strapping the canvas bucket
to my back the autumn I climbed
wooden, triangular ladders, masked
as migrant worker against
the poison.

Tonight I find you, a leopard,
straddling
limb & limb, over limb,
where no sweetness
can be added
to you.

This Morning on the Early Ferry

> *...wings rushing down the mountainside*
> *or flames clinging to a torched village.*
> **-Agha Shahid Ali**

Did I leave you out of nighttime
prayers once too often, Noman, for your family
to postpone telling you for a month
that your father died in Pakistan?

They must have thought it best
for you to miss the rituals,
the grieving, hoping
not to interrupt
your studies.

Just before that sad news I wrote to Shahid to say I saw you
on campus, the weight of your workload, the world,
(you saw hundreds killed in the streets of Karachi)
curving your back
like the black-crowned night Heron.

You were my lone
connection to the geography,
politics, tragedy of Kashmir.

This morning on the early ferry across Boston Harbor
I saw the sun
rise out of shoreline trees,

color spreading over the sea as if from saffron strands.

I know only the tinge
of your sorrow.

Ode to New York City

Prelude: **A View of the City**

Approaching by train, heading under the skyline, she summed New York up, "The wounded city." Ironic, the shock to see Ground Zero out a hotel window, I mean the desk attendant said we'd have a view of the city, but this? (Vanished?) Cranes & Klieg lights, steam shovels shoveling the never-ending mass grave. Frank O'Hara could still hear the Third Avenue El after it was torn down, & maybe that's how I prefer to remember the architecture: a sound, the way Andrew Wilson compared the Towers to a tuning fork, & Oh, the pitch still reverberating through the universe such measure of the magnitude of our mourning.

The Sky Transformed

Need for gaiety when the first day of the weekend is spent,
unexpectedly, in a kind of silent
mourning at Ground Zero,
& the meager language
we muster remains
mostly internal,
visceral.
So the next day get up early to take the Staten Island Ferry,
not to get anywhere, because it's free,
& Baudelaire praised contemplation
of a ship, especially one in motion,
as mysterious & infinite.

With Ellis Island in the near distance, where my father said they changed
our name from Fitzgibbons,
we are poor immigrants among all the passengers,
looking over our shoulders reminding us again
of the disaster down there,
where the Towers were,
as much from the hole in the sky
as the one in the ground.
It's difficult to pull oneself up out of mourning into gaiety in one fell
swoop.
I could have used the dream where my Soul became visible
to my daughter only
so that I had to look through her eyes
on the bus where my Soul was a rectangular piece of glass
hovering in the air
in the aisle
& pressed within it was a rose, *Eros*.
So, of course, we head to Gotham Book Mart on 47th St.
where we know we'll find gems
like a cheap copy of Apollinaire's erotic writings,
& Baudelaire's **Intimate Journals**.
There's nothing like French wit to help bring one up:
"She was as red as a beet, her bosom
was shaking, but she was at a loss for words."
"I am sick of France; chiefly because everyone is like Voltaire."
Frank O'Hara joins us, too,
when his **Selected Poems** opens all by itself
to "Poem Read at Joan Mitchell's," when we're already on our way
to 83rd Street to meet Barney Rosset,
the legend, who published Lawrence & Miller & Olson.
But not before tramping through the desert of wealth in the Upper Sixties

& Seventies making me thirsty, making me wish
out loud for a Champagne bar
like the one that rescued me
from my hangover after the Rauschenberg show at the Whitney,
when all of a sudden this little gelato place on 73rd & Madison turns
into none other, (words in fine print,)
than a Champagne bar. Ah! Via Quadronno!
We share a glass of Gavi de Gavi for $13.50, which does the trick, getting
us out of the residential desert
into the art world between 83rd & 84th where Janos Gat greets us at his
gallery
with a glass of red wine telling us Barney & Astrid
are in the other room ready to greet us with smiles & handshakes & photographs from the war in the 40's & a story
about Joan Mitchell when Barney lived with her
in the south of France & recognized it was time,
that her work had gotten to a point
where they could go home to New York
with Pollock & de Kooning, Motherwell & Kline,
but responded she couldn't, her oeuvre too large & vast to move.
Barney offered to carry it all all
by himself
on the lone condition she marry him.
A few years later, after their formal relationship ended,
O'Hara wrote his wonderful poem, ironically one he would have made as
long
as friendship
could last if he could have written a poem that long.
Choko came by with her cell phone, effusive ebullience, & exotic look.
The young publisher, Scott Korb, as thrilled
to meet the legend as I was as thrilled to meet the legend.

went out with us afterward for a bottle of Cahors,
the "Black Wine of France," where we shared
stories of coming to writing,
our trip to Cannes, his living in Ireland,
the link between intelligence & consciousness,
intuition & the unconscious, the reiteration of his mission
to publish what is earnest & honest over cynical & ironic,
reminding me of my distaste for Voltaire.
We parted in front of Nicola's on 84th with a firm handshake,
a willingness to face the events of today
with a language of risk & metamorphosis,
& one unforgettable image recalled from that morning
of the row of pollarded sycamores on 43rd with branches reaching
into the sky transformed
into the grieving hands of Grünewald.

An Echo of the Silence of the Dead

We took our sadness for the world to the orchard.
Nothing but green. Slowly the red, the black bark. Ashes
of our sadness began to lift.
Apple trees absorb
grief, quietly.
Off in the distance we imagined a castle.
Red blanket on long green grass, cloudless blue.
We didn't need to talk,
thoughts too similar to exchange.
The "Keep Out" sign had made no sense to us
at a time like this. Just hours before the autumnal equinox,
we saw shadows move.
Two little yellow butterflies rose up in dance,
a thoroughly interdependent prelude
to sexual encounter.
She wondered what it would be like to sleep out here,
answering her own question with "Cold,"
the word continuing through the orchard, an echo
of the silence of the dead.
The near fruit, the distant invisible
stars, with us as one.

If Blood Fuels the Engine

If blood fuels the engine
of the sentence...
Write desire.
To combine, one eye on the slant of the sun, the other
on the living,
recording the annunciation,
listening to an 11-year-old daughter say,
"Nonetheless...,"
knowing, herself,
it is
one word.

Gathering to myself,
for myself, & loved ones ingredients
for this week's soup, whatever is at hand
(our own rule of thumb is a house is not a home without
an onion,) heat the oil on a Saturday
or Sunday, add the onion -

the AIDS patient on the front page of the *NYT* has sores indistinguishable, without a closer look, from tattoos, makes his way into the imaginings of the poet writing about food -abundance, availability of... or, Christ, even the day before, Saturday, November 7th the photograph of Bosnian refugees stranded at the last minute outside Sarajevo, which Kathleen compared to the devotion of some Renaissance Master, say, Andrea del Sarto, his *Madonna and Child with the Young St. John, St.*

Elizabeth and Two Angels, or if it had been colorized, revealing all the terror, anguish, & exhaustion of these Bosnian refugees, damned, captive, exiled, as they are, the picture might have rivaled the staging of Raphael's, *The Fire in the Borgo.*

      Two Idaho potatoes, scrubbed, unpeeled, three stalks celery, whatever, nonetheless, the vegetable bin offers: mustard greens from Martha's farm in Maryland, a tomato, from god knows where, very old carrots, which would have been a disgrace to discard, the same number of sweet potatoes on their last legs, causing the girls & their mother & I to address the issue of the importance of tuber & root this time of year, each year nearing Thanksgiving, Veterans Day is Wednesday when they (now) begin reading
names
at
noon
today & will around the clock reaching upward of...
         My first visit Sept. 23, 1990
         knowing two people there, a cousin born the same day

as I was,
& a friend from high school I bumped into on the playing field Melanie Klein says (the sun slants into the soup) athletic striving is a drive back to the womb, oh!
& I found the names
         Richard Gray
         Steven Donaldson

                          remembered my mother had
         spoken

of being in the same hospital room with "Rittie's" mother. I remember him, later, that slightly crossed eye. His grandmother & my grandfather were sister & brother.
Steve, I'd no notion that you were born a week or so before us. That you would have been 44 the day I arrived to honor you, that I'd find your death date on your birthday...!
The Wall, then
comforts us, as walls will,
my wife sleeps soundly next to me in the small upstairs bedroom,
through her now I return having given up athletics that final (intrauterine) year, here the sentence, if blood fuels
the engine, strives, here the cautious volley of...

    the word across
    the bow of
    the newly fallen.

                             There is so
                       much

I like the dirt
grows things,
the chervil I had to add, & ubiquitous salt, except there, in Srebrenica, where we find out only now, people survived an entire winter on pear tree bark & melted snow,
the AIDS patient, all sores recognizable at a closer look, wishing life could be rolled back
to the womb, I woke

           this morning wondering what experiences I might have
to write to

validate my desire to, to word. Add water. The sun comes in today like an
eternal
column
to balance
the rest of life on.
Wake to, Robert, provide.

A Bruegel in Vienna for a Friend in Kiev

Nothing reluctant, the singing,
the kissing, the blind
love in rhythm,
in sync with
ox-bladder bagpipe.
It's Oktoberfest, everyone hopped up.
The oak in the foreground still holds on
to leaves, but a fallen jug handle foreshadows
the next day. Two children
offer each other the purity of open,
empty hands. The church at road's end
in admiration of its harvest of soles. The best
peasant blood dances disregarding the obvious
proximity to skeletal remains,
& particles of earth rising
before us too fine for us
to see.

Cavafy's Men

Talking with a couple of young men,
as if they were Cavafy's,
at a time when the local paper
prints an article claiming it's safe
for travelers to return to Lebanon,
full-color photos of the azure water in the harbor of Sidon.
Speedboats at anchor.
Marble ruins
of Jupiter's Temple at Baalbek.
Yet, how their stories diverge.
One returned there during the '82 war,
& four years later carried his infant nephew
across town during fighting between
Phalangists & leftists.
The other stayed here in the States.
Even though the young men of his generation still wear hair long,
& profess the area's most radical views,
he hates all talk of politics.
Prefers travel
to New York, Las Vegas, L.A.
Last year he returned home for the first time
in a long while, bringing back a bottle of wine
made from grapes in the Bekaa Valley,
which heightened the joy
of telling the story. It didn't surprise me at all

to learn he made a point of visiting
the remains of the Roman
amphitheater near his home in Batroun.

Before Each Sacrifice

He counted twice before
bringing down a tree to turn it
into charcoal.
First, it was a living thing.
Second, it might have hidden powers.
The brief pause
before each sacrifice
assured Nassir avoided harm.
When the lone date palm in his village
of Betaaboura, Lebanon was destroyed
he knew the man
would come to grief.
A neighbor, disturbed that bats feasted on the fruit,
reluctant to cut down the tree his father planted
fifty years ago,
let his uncle's son convince him it was in the way.
The cousin drilled the hole
to add the poison.
Within a month: a withered silhouette.
As bad luck had it, while ploughing in the field
the tiller caught the man's pant leg
chewing down to flesh to ankle bone.
He still walks,
but with difficulty,

five steel rods clanging
rigid in the limb.

In North Lebanon

Nassir is going back to his thousand trees.
Olives, ancient, & revered as the grape.
"Acorn," for building. Almond.
One, in particular, dead for ten years, only the black
trunk left too distant from the house
for use.
Nassir began to notice a change,
of color, or something else inside the tree.
He told his father he believed it would come back to life.
Now, it flowers.
The whole time
he's telling the story of the miracle
almond tree, I'm picturing the sky above a thousand trees,
imagining the ground
as the patch of earth Bonnard asked his nephew from his deathbed
to change from green to yellow.
Other than the painting,
I've never seen an almond tree.
The only olive,
at the Botanic Garden
in Washington.
Nassir knows a place far
from his village, difficult
to trek to, where the stones bear all the earmarks
of a Time before Law,

before civilization.

His tone of voice revealed he found Peace there.

Providence

for **Manuel Pedroso**

Some believe the friend is waiting.
Across the river,
down Water St. to Wickenden, a fortuitous
turn on to Brook. You waited there,
Manuel Pedroso, ready to greet us
under the shelves
of a hundred
Madonnas.

I waved when I came in,
complimenting you on your market.
At eighty, you must know places
like this don't exist anymore.
You've had to steer a good, Portuguese, navigational course,
not only for your own longevity, but for the store's,
& Maria's, wife of how many years,
who greeted us warmly, gave us

chestnuts to eat, & doubled
the plastic bags for wine I bought
across the street.
I promised not to wax nostalgic if I wrote anything when we left
for our room that night back on Weybosset St.
Get the hell out, Nostalgia!

It was only a coincidence. So what
if Manuel Pedroso makes the best homemade wine in Providence!

What if he did teach me
the word for Nightingale – *Rouxinal* – my guess
is neither of us was waiting; it was only a coincidence
we took full advantage of because we're open,
& value all the moments left to us,
tossing them in with bags
full of wine, sardines,
cornbread, fruit, inspired
words, kindness.

Besides, I've had more than just one
Portuguese friend,
my friend.

Stones Trees Names

The last day of February unfolds,
an illuminated manuscript
the unexpected ice storm makes of it.
Surrounding lines, & angles gather reflected light at every turn,
bestow an intensified color.

At noon
I go to the Jewish cemetery on the outskirts of town.
Here, at the beginning of the century, the Jews of the city found land
to bury their dead.

I'm welcome here.
Trees reach down, offer comfort.
Headstones covered with a cross
between haloes & yarmulkes of ice & light.

Perhaps it's a scrolled Torah the day unrolls into.
Max Locomovitch, truly loved by his children.
Frances Mary Science, honored & respected.

I always viewed Jacob van Ruysdael's, *The Jewish Cemetery*, somehow out
of sync
with the rest of his landscape oeuvre. Until now.
The stones, the trees, the names,
the lives all return to the same

framed space.
There are echoes here,
unheard. Pictures of forgotten
smiles. I can't get over the absolute empathy
of the trees. Pathetic fallacy? Ashes!
I simply want to praise this space, the solace
provided by the dead.

Near Two Rivers

an epithalamium for **Nicole & Gary Leet**

That's sort of the way I want to write this, the way
the bee rolled this morning, abandoning
method, just rolling over
& over
in the calyx of the beach rose, immersed in pollen.
An invitation out of the blue to a wedding of a distant/close cousin of
hers
I'd met only once before, but I remember the time.
It was in Rhode Island.
The ceremony
took place at the bride's house on the bank of a river which rose up in the
heat, the river rose up in the heat of the day in Connecticut, hung there,
a second river
in the air,
it was really something to see. I kept looking
at it in awe. The second river was even more intriguing
than the one below it,
but the cool air came wind-borne
from the one below. The huge oak tree where the couple stood
above all the extended roots in the ground, I could hear the roots growing
during the ceremony, gave shade to those in attendance.
Dance was the nature of the day.
The day danced.
Listen, grandmother, did you ever in your wildest dreams, oh,

how I would love to have eavesdropped on your wildest
dreams, grandmother, when you took me
to New York City in 1954, would you
have thought, you know, the six
movies we saw, the paper
airplanes thrown out
the twenty-something floor windows of the Taft,
would you, could you, grandmother, have imagined
that your grandson, that little boy who cried in the plane
because others, the rest of the family couldn't go along to the Big Apple,
but said it was the sun
in his eyes,
when you asked, grandmother,
& Radio City Music Hall was by far
the highlight of the trip, grandmother, the legs,
the black lines of stockings from buttock curve to ankle,
America's version of the Moulin Rouge & Paris, dearest grandmother,
who showed me there was more to the world than the world
I knew at the time, could you have imagined that I would attend
the wedding of a couple
where the groom was lucky enough to marry a Rockette?
Really, grandmother in heaven, it happened!
Yesterday, in Connecticut!
Near two rivers!
Just as the groom placed the ring on his soon-to-be wife's finger I saw
a kingfisher, bird of good omen, swim through the river hung suspended
in sultry air.
How many rivers are in heaven?
Heaven's rivers modeled on this one,
this two. You could say Nicole & Gary are modeled on

heaven's rivers. Go ahead, grandmother, say it,
"Nicole & Gary are modeled on
heaven's rivers."

Border

Long ignored corner of ground I see
disjunctive
to the universe,
blessed in solitude,
inviting covenant.

Rain eases over leaves, blackens
trunks, becomes then, river.
Inward river I've found,
cresting.

To time which holds
to stones, add knowledge & memory,
which run along pulse or desire.
Pulse & desire.

Basquiat Never Babysat

Basquiat never babysat.
Probably didn't have much
use for Bouguereau, languid white flesh
in French landscape, even though they spoke
the same language.

If he painted kids, he painted kids
with all the trademarks © of his streetwise
Brooklyn accent in black marginal stick-figure outlines
magic marker Soul.
Kids crowned kings.

Or perhaps sisters & a playmate transformed
into ballerina dancers at either ends,
& up & over the jump rope, inserting the shadow
of their own ancestral Harlem
elder looking on.

Replenishings

A true thoroughfare,
rivaling the Boulevards of Paris: catching all the green
lights from Alexandria-Arlington-Falls Church, Virginia along Route 7.

Never happen.

The water the air the light the %ages we're made of.

The brass tacks we need to keep the black cloth up on the underside
of my grandfather's white Naugahyde chair. No
sooner put this down than friends
& I visiting the Museum
of African Art discover headrests & chairs totally, ornamentally, (ritually)
down to brass tacks.
Gold. Nails.
I've lugged that heirloom in & out of over ten living spaces.
Very unlike a cross.

Addendum of Melanie Klein where she states that our caretakers are integrated
into ourselves. Best know this: others in us.

Dreams: 1. Excavation of the boxer. Beuys figure slumped against sagging ropes,
dead more than knocked out, in fact, inanimate old rags stuffed into

nylon become Hans Bellmer form.

Next frame: half-submerged corpse in earth.
Next: covered in plastic.
Next: tools to sift for skeletal details.
Next: risen clean,
a work of art whose
next performance is to fight no fight.

2. My touch changes your demeanor.

To wake to you to March to Spring. I paint in dream all night, a true
ideogram in blue, silver, & ground, image & word combined: *Your New
Trees* with Fate standing to the side applauding her thin white hands.

So heightened my desire for you.
its voice says, I want to live.

3. Snow piled high along the roadsides. Call to friends in the vicinity.
(Those we so often prefer to ourselves.)
Welcome response & plans dispersed out of sequence: You & your twin
walk hand-in-hand out
of the cottage (or out of the photograph
I saw for the first time a month ago.)
You point out worn shingles within reach of the glow of the kitchen
window.
Night. You show her where the work of art is essential. / / / / /
It ought to be right there in the recesses of the corner walls.
If not a landscape
based on surrounding mountains, then the light of a slide
projected from the woods

a short distance away, where at night both of you,

together or alone, (Beauty is
that voracious) might enter,
a funnel of pure light,
safely, without anyone seeing a shadow
cast from you.

4. I'm flipping through a micro-fiche Rolodex looking for something by Blake.
Turn immediately to it: "Love one in love." -Blake.
I wake to her.
Shining through the film.
It's early April when the Christmas cactus gives a second crack
at the light.

& there she is in her blue
bathrobe adding enough water to force
more flowering.

In fact, next time that's all the tree
& festivities we'll need:
> Cactus as tree suspended from ceiling.
> Her, as virgin, Madonna or angel reaching up above it.
> Water, the silver star.
> Flowers, electricity.
> Today, the earliest opening of the present.

Breath is the measure. (Then, death)? *Is?*

In the middle of the lengthy night, without sound
of diesel-fuel-blue horses,
but that of the sky hatching new stars,
I get up from space where constant praise belongs.
Next you in bed.
Once downstairs, recollection of a time **not** spent together:
Saw a thousand things diminish
in importance.

Sun remains among stones in a wooden box.

Air, nothing, if not for you to breathe.

My life, useless, unless in that space
of constant praise,
I return to the watch: your dream in my reality.

It's Sunday, leftover red
wine good enough in cups made in the German Democratic Republic.

It's water & light I'm going on today, that's all. Clarity
of the combination
brightens everything in between. Those trees,
what they do, but travel vertically on light & water & a few charitable
stones.

That day when you were a drop of the sun's blood.
That river, of which we had no need
for further depth.

Wet, that is, without an Heraclitean nature to impede appreciation of
pure sensuality,

you sat down, mid-stream,
underpants eventually matching imprint
of stones & flesh
in algae.

Or, to abide the fragments,
you were a flame on the Fourth of July in another country erecting
an independence
no proposition
or possible future
guise of desire
could unhinge.

(Self-contained image of the fish, riding the back of the horse,
from its phallic head to its vulvar
caudal fin at the cave
of Pech-Merle.)

We are the carnal,
marrow, alive in the bones
of the earth.

We rode each other across the entire country.

Along the ten kilometer trek, we didn't know what the farmers had
planned
to grow, but saw what was up: a fine outcropping

of flints.

The [Untitled] black paintings
built up like skyscrapers
on newsprint by Rauschenberg burn up
in the basement of the mind
in the Stable Gallery in NYC (where he performed that Herculean labor
to clean
police horse quarters in order to exhibit the work.)
The yellow,
the red
simplicity
of fire the spontaneous combustion imagination survives in.

The hieratic stance of the wounded Assyrian Lioness Margo is studying
for the History of Art. I test her. She gets 23-2200 BC right.
& the Venus of Willendorf is, again, older
than I thought. The importance
of her sculpted labial
(vertical)
line.

As well, the importance of the other, perhaps,
more often [?],
unsculpted
(aniconic)
stones.

Thorough. (Fair). She is cleaning something. Now!

Mornings her visage solves all dilemmas.

Her body, the engine of day.
Without needing to verify

specifics,
she is a constellation,
at home, in The Milky Way.

Up here where time can be thrown down into the mouth
of space, & damned, if today the sun isn't a bridge (a bride) across the entire abyss
of the self.

& the heart counts itself among the expanse of nature.

The male Muses call, too, - ancestral fathers & caretakers, young brothers, rivals,
friends. Last afternoon sun, blood filling the labial folds & injured
cry of clitoral climax timed with the telephone.
He wants to know if he's interrupting anything – supper or –
no, no interruption at all.
There is room for
the interest,
room for the far-away
companion –
she comes in in the shared red
air, shy, confident animal (Fauve) to nuzzle & stroke -*yes, we are all right,
the celebration was grand & you were missed, yet felt present.* Room, again,
in
the light

& spring air of breath for another
[this] work's occasion.

The welcome yellow light. A sort of mango
light of Yeats's *Mango Trick,* where the self-contained morning begins to
spread out beyond itself, (there's love
coming through one bedroom window) shoots out leaves & limbs, gathers lianas
& insects, makes inroads of roots
& produces,
again, with the help, finally, of a fierce yellow light, new flesh.
Good morning, Love, look. Would you (light?) like to go out in it, or
stay, perched on the branch of the bed?

The Three Trees

At its furthest inland reaches the sea prepares,
next the salt-marsh bank, new mud,
where unseen, a broad-winged bird
plants in careful strokes,
tracks,
like oriental willows.

Lifting off
one year after Saskia's passing,
parallel to the low-level City, it enters
the center of the sky in Rembrandt's, *The Three Trees,*

which, in turn, will be cut
& burnished, straightened, & assembled with their transverse beams-
drypoint & burin gouged,
ten years later, into
The Three Crosses.

Lovers hidden in the thicket,
lamentations upon the stones.

Amsterdam

Resist the big Dutch women, one can't.
Adriana van Heusden, draped in her linen

apron covering the ermine trim of her jacket,
selects from the display of fish in the Amsterdam

market. In Emmanuel de Witte's painting, the hand
of the fishmonger favors a perfect cod. Haddock, salmon,

sole tied from tail to mouth, crab, a ray.
One is surprised here, 1661, that

the Atlantic is common ground, yet the Boston basin
is older than cod & six hundred million years ago settled

next to Africa. Burlap awnings shade fish from the sun.
A lantern swings under the commotion.

Canvas billows in the port. Adriana's daughter
stares from behind her into the future, will

continue a tradition from Rembrandt & Vermeer
through the big women of Willem de Kooning.

Death as Intruder of Solitude

It made all sense the world all,
unmade all sense the world all,
the things of the world all
upside down at the time
of death.

Which you & Beckmann knew.
Your own painting, you told me, from a dream,
what else could the sky be, but a blue mule
staring down in sympathy?
Of course, Beckmann placed his fish
in the night sky,
out of reach
of water.

Further anomalies occur.
That small oil of his, stored for years
in the basement vault of the Fogg Museum,
a still life, its curator pointed out,
when she brought me down to see it, is not still,
includes fire,
of all things, with green leaves

   supporting what is probably a huge tulip blossom towering
out of a clay pot near the stove glowing

black in the warehouse, in 1945,
where Beckmann painted right
under the nose of his German countrymen in the occupied
city of Amsterdam.

Cutler, Maine: *Fruits de Mer*

Tourists don't make it much beyond Schoodic Point
by car, or if by sail, rest at anchor,
turn round at Somes Sound,
our only Atlantic fjord,
then head home.

Makes a place like Cutler seem off the map,
invisible,
without a correct set of navigational charts.

We only know the place
through the machinations
of a scraggly Irishman who settled
in Machias some thirty years ago
below Bad Little Falls, knowing it
as the site of the first naval battle of the Revolution,
knowing only good friends would travel that far
for one more wedding celebration.

We got Downeast a day ahead of time.
Under the first sun in weeks.
Highest temperatures all year.

Hungry for shellfish, ocean,
& each other.

Clams dug from gravely soil make them clean.
Without a market for the product in town we dealt directly
      with the men bending over their catch on the flats.

My wife went barefoot.
All one heard the whole way out at low tide
were the moaning, orgasmic sounds mud
causes oozing through a woman's toes.
Oh! Oooh! Which was OK with me as long as she kept close,
the tide long in space, long in time,
Cutler, first port on the Bay of Fundy tidal range.

If tourists do make it past Schoodic,
past Petit Manan Bar, Cape Split, few,
if any, walk out on the endless reach of flats
at Cutler. Suspicion reigned,
momentarily.
Diggers turned to size us up,
then went back to business.
They recognized Venus
emerging, imagined
her dressed
in mud,
& practically
gave the fruits of their hard-won livelihood away.

When Ivar Bardsen Gave his Chorography

When the old Greenlander,
Ivar Bardsen, gave his chorography,
pointing out Iceland
was seven days sailing due west from Norway,
& that from there Greenland
was two days & two nights away, warning
the ice down from the northern recesses
of the ocean had adhered closely
to Gunnbjorn's Rocks,

that those wishing to sail directly
from Bergen in Norway to Greenland
must sail twelve nautical miles
south of the promontory of Reykiannaes,
westward to the high land
of Greenland, the inhabited part
lying most to the east called Skage Fjord,

& that at the harbor of Bere Fjord
there was a great whirlpool called the Whale's Whirlpool
into which the whales entered as the tide went out,
it was then the middle of the fourteenth century,
& it would be over two hundred & fifty years
before Henry Hudson would sail due west

with a copy of Bardsen's directions in his possession.

This Afric Temple of the Whale

> *In this Afric Temple of the Whale I leave you, reader, and if you be a Nantucketer, and a whaleman, you will silently worship there.*
> **-H.M., M.D.**

The kind of awe Melville knew, the whale
washed up on the beach on a Sunday
morning, the mass of Americans
beginning to gather 'round it,
more out of curiosity
than anything else,
the spectacle!

At the same time keeping their distance, repelled
by the smell. While kids held their noses,
we walked close up.
I mean for me it smelled like Gloucester.
Redfish processing plants
on the inner harbor
side of the Fort.

Long decayed skin gone,
the next layer, a pearly
white.

One would have to be a fool not to think of the minute description in his
novel
of the "Leviathan."

One such fool told me you could hardly tell
which end was which, "No,"
I countered, "I know which end is which,"
which shut him down,
what with everyone
in this country required
to agree, especially
strangers.

Massive oblong cliff
of forehead
missing.

Instead, what previously encased the nasal canal
revealed an amazing elongation,
a trunk matching
an elephant's!

Miraculous organ, at once windpipe, at once spout,
Melville found analogous to the source
of all that is ponderous & profound
in man, calling it the Fountain.

The only fin visible at that point
of decomposition ground down
to a double set of ivory bones
like tusks, bringing it closer
yet again to its distant
cousin on land.

The mysterious lump of sturdy material, detached,
intact, disguised in all spectators' eyes
as the giant rock it rested on,
was in fact its lower
jaw.

Past Ventry

One's movement in crossing
should be in keeping with the landscape.
This land, a stronghold, the Blasket Islands
keeping the ocean itself at bay, the woman
here, Irish-speaking descendent
looking after us at Tig Mollai's,
solid as a dolmen.

Osiris

Where the past shall be a source of light,
heart & blood are a river of Memory.

I cross into the dark trees,
experiencing a dream in which
it is my task to find a man
reported drowned. A path at once
familiar & unknown ascends
a mountain through juniper
shrub, tall spruce.
January sun's low arc
seems to quicken the journey.
Direct attention as I walk,
concurrent with a view of the entire scene,

I am without fear.
At the summit the sky comes close.
Here is the Lake of Heaven,
source of the Nile. A body
I presume dead is buoyant, supine
in the water, feet wrapped
like the tail of a fish, arms also,
fingers only out from his sides
are fins. Ochre painted face,
a wooden, weathered mask,

old, yet representing youth, his crown
forms the bow-sprit of a boat.

An arc of water pours
from the mouth of Osiris,
a fountain to which a woman
approaches in white robes
from the shore at the right,
a white rectangle, hieroglyphic
temple looming in the background.
Isis, arriving to remember Osiris
with a fig branch, return
him to the white sepulchre,
establish that,
MEMORY IS THE LIFE OF THE DEAD.

I Wanted to Get it Down: A Comparable Image

I wanted to get it down.
They scaled the heights.
I was on the ground, in futile pursuit of Eros.
Five long ropes reaching the sidewalk.
The others didn't see it, those executives,
men of power, thinking a clean window is clear vision.
Look at them: circus performers, the Salvadoran window-washers.
Their technique? Once on the roof attach grappling hooks
& straps, the one-board seat,
then in a leap of faith
hoist over lion-headed cornice, & hang
over the abyss,
momentarily.
Kick one foot against the marble wall, & plunge
black rubber stoppers against the pane.
Spray chemical, wave
squeegee back & forth & round.
Unstop stoppers, & swing
down the eleventh,
tenth,
ninth-floor windows finished in under six minutes.

Spectatorship entails considerable awe.
Five men, but I couldn't help think of the women,
absent.

What of Love between them?
It must be Love to risk their lives.
Sappho
compared girls to apples,
observing how fruit in top-most branches remained
unpicked.
What I sought when I left the house this morning was a comparable image
to the dream I once had, when agonized between two women
in my life, riding a bicycle
down a dirt road,
suddenly blinded, my glasses clogged: one lens filled with honey,
the other mustard,
two ladybugs caught inside,
trying to get out.
Sappho called Eros the bittersweet.
These men, higher than rows of honey locusts in the park a block away,
the ones staring into the abyss,
risking their lives.

The Unmentionable

The kid, bright, expressing interest
in writing, mostly in silence,
while his father & I drank,
listening to Cuban music.
The father happy
to be away,
the son secretly
longing to return.
Three men.
The kid, first-gen-Cuban-American,
soon graduating from secondary school
with honors, the Cuban exile
& I, well, parlaying
questions & answers & banter the whole night,
the music, the rum, into one
formidable experience.

So the next day I sought the kid out
to give him my copy
of Hemingway's
Complete Short Stories,
the edition named after the author's
retreat on the kid's ancestral island.

It's taken ten years to get another copy.

It arrived by mail yesterday, & today
I took it down to the seawall,
where the wind
opened it to
"The Sea Change,"
that piece of sublimated anger
in which neither the words "sea,"
nor "Lesbian,"
are mentioned, yet the latter
subject covers the pages like a cool sheet
flung across a hot hotel bed.

Straight to "Hills like White Elephants,"
where both sides of the DMZ
of abortion at that time,
drawn along gender lines,
is mapped out
without mentioning the word.

Perhaps tonight,
I'll read "A Clean Well-Lighted Place,"
drinking a few cups, wondering again
how he got that language
to work the miracle of
the unmentionable.

The Dream Bread

The impact
of the image struck to the core.
House of the Chaste Lovers in Pompeii,
buried under ash & lava, named
for the fresco
showing both lovers clothed.
The building is actually a bakery.
A fragment shows a rooster
pecking at a pomegranate.
Last night I kneaded the dream bread,
filling it with carrots & seeds.
I meant it
as a gift to her,
an offering, trying to root out any
underlying
discord between us.

House of the Chaste Lovers

…beyond your own life build the great arch
of unimagined bridges.
- **Rilke**

Snow-tattered April,
but that's alright, so are my clothes.
I don't have to wear Sunday-best on Wednesday.
Threads of snow dizzying around like stray helixes purifying the air.
I always look on the bright side, worrying
only over the irredeemable,
the irretrievable,
or like the fresco stolen from the House of the Chaste Lovers in Pompeii,
the fragment only recently returned,
some experts say,
irreparably damaged.

It shows a rooster pecking at a pomegranate,
surely filled with erotic symbolism.
The fear, not to have a second chance,
or change directions, or be able to salvage
a few more years. What the dream does so well.
For instance, during a recent visit home,
while she slept in the room next to us,
I dreamt our daughter chose a notebook
from the shelf in our bedroom,
the cover miraculously
portraying the image
of the Tao.

Later that week those same shelves disappeared,
everything in the dream
bedroom,
gone.
But I saw myself,
in the exact spot where my old oak writing table stood
for so long, hovering over a single plank of wood,
stretched like a bridge across
two stacks of cinder blocks,
writing.

Just this morning another dream proclaimed
its indispensable role like an ancient
oracle: "Exhumation of Life."

Nature or Civilization

I'm going to force this poem to start with the image
of all colors gathering
in the sky erecting the arc of a black rainbow. With luck,
close it, with a bolt of lightning
from a dream.
Clouds accentuate the greatness of the world.
It's not that I want to see them,
the rows of immobile mobile homes by the side of the railroad track.
From the windows of the new fast train
one has to wonder
whether these structures, their inhabitants
aren't closer to nature
than civilization?
The attractive contours of the architecture of the poor
have disappeared since William Carlos Williams noted them.
Soon the sandy Rhode Island soil,
scrub pines, all the way down
to New London osprey,
red-winged blackbirds, the smidgen
of sea.
Those homes stay in my head, returning
uncanny, metamorphosed into anthills, wasp nests.
The residents,
whose relationship to the train is one of avoiding
intermittent noise, without movement, change, wandering…

Sudden feeling of thankfulness to America which allows this bare-bones subsistence
with a shake of its huge head & lack of compassion, not wanting
to know a single soul
in the trailer park, their pain, or pain any one of them could inflict
on each other in such tight quarters,
& do.
Kandinsky felt all means sacred
called forth by inner necessity.
My own lack of compassion for those dwelling there
is in stark contrast to anything sacred. Make it compulsory
that everyone in America
who makes more than
one-hundred & fifty-nine thousand
four-hundred & twenty-three dollars & sixty-three cents
a year, clean
the grease off at least one trailer-park stove
a year, thoroughly!
By New Rochelle it's all
barbed wire & drums
of toxic waste, high rises low
rises, & no one on the street. The dream
of April 5th says, "The tall virtues are patience,
mercy, & immediacy."
By Wilmington the sign reads
Guaranteed Destruction of Personal Records.
I wonder
what was going on with me
when, forgetting my monthly rail pass
I said to myself, "I forgot

my past today."
In Washington my favorite trees,
the ones that bloom first
because of the sun's reflection
against I.M.Pei's East Wing, the ones
illuminating Jean Arp's steel sculptures,
are in flower.

& because the curator
doesn't show
at the appointed time
I find the Senufo wooden bowl
& the Dogon stool at Miya Gallery
on E Street. Greetings, Vernard Gray.
The sky in the most recent dream, little different than yesterday
or today's
with sheets of rain threatening in the distance,
yet only the dream sky induces
the flash of lightning
to materialize. We run for cover.
I find a series of caves, first stone, then snow, then wood, a kind of oak veneer
in an old room.
I want to make love to her in each one,
but we move on too fast, or the dream moves on
too fast to satisfy my desire.
Only upon waking does the dream
come true, within the cave
of her flesh bolt upright.

So, with good fortune, or Fate
the dream lightning is not the end
of the poem, but denouement.

There is a Fig Tree

There is a fig tree filled with clarity,
bare, in the brief winter
of Paros, or north,
in Salonika.

It practically disappears against the blue sky,
returns lit up within
night's blackness.

There's the fork of the loins
of Dionysos. There's the carnal
remains, bones left in the hills
by Bacchantes.

Summers without silence.
Wasps hissing, battling for figs.

In this one anonymous photograph,
like a fragment torn
from *The Anthology*, it's without ornament,
not without promise.

Plenty of solid ground to spread out on, head
placed next the trunk like a discarded
ceremonial stone, heart,
near gnarled root.

Jade Cicada

Go ahead, one of you who still loves,
place the tongue-amulet in my mouth
at the time of death.
Jade cicada,
carved with great difficulty & care.
Insect musician,
instrumentalist.
A tradition
traced back four millennia in China.
The name for jade is *yu*.
Food of the spirits.
The Western version of the word is from the Spanish,
piedra de la ijada,
stone of the loins.

II
That I might drum,
communicate with you, the living,
as the cicada will,
when the sun is strong enough to reach
underground.
When the dead grin at their own
folly, & earth puts on new flesh: drum

thoracic drum, drum oracular outcry,
drum love's drum.

Fate's rock-ribbed drum,
drum no plaintive drum, drum instant
of desire, drum return where love once accompanied…
Drum thoracic drum, drum oracular outcry,
drum love's drum…

III. from *Streets for Two Dancers*

...if there are words there are two dancers...
— WCWilliams

To turn the threatening future into a fulfilled "now," the only desirable telepathic miracle, is a work of bodily presence of mind. Primitive epochs, when such demeanor was part of man's daily husbandry, provided him with the most reliable instrument of divination: the naked body.

— **Walter Benjamin**

Mass Transit

Up High St. past the old brick Chadwick Lead Works, where at an angle toward the harbor a large gargoyle holding a flagpole in the center of its skull guards the outskirts of Boston's financial district, across to Batterymarch, where at either end of rush hour you can still walk in the middle of the street, as if it were a back-alley sister to London or Dublin, over to Milk & Post Office Square on this blustery November day, beggars more visible than company presidents, & office girls' skirts funneling the wind twelve flights to the center of their beings. Beyond the puckered smokers, anyone offering the slightest smile makes you wonder what's wrong. At State the subway entrance smells like a cross between an opened crypt & a sewer as I slide down the Orange Line all the way to work.

Boots & Divination

> *In the most elementary hierophany* EVERYTHING IS DECLARED
>
> **-Mircea Eliade**

Under asphalt on Batterymarch the clang of cobblestones rose up as if under iron shoes of horses instead of my boots & divination. A few days later I looked around for the hard evidence. Real joy in discovering the alley separating the Royal Arcanum Building erected in 1877, & the present Charrette. Nothing but a great grid of cobbles undisturbed, in situ, like a set of molars when the street was the mouth of commerce.

Communicating Vessels

It was as if things & utterance merged. Red delphinium vibrated behind our talk influenced by French Burgundy. The friend called soul & fertility of soil equal. It happened in a flash. On a street given over almost entirely to fashion. For a second poetry clasped presence & memory together with the strength of sinew. Language: direct descendant of the senses. Love rose, a sea in the bloodstream.

Write Naked

Initially, the need for transition suddenly fragments flow collage, listen to Schoenberg.

White Dog (of Death)

Believe it, I was in the same room with Brassai. OK, an auditorium. I was also a month old when he & Picasso discussed differing styles of graffiti in Paris, Rome, Barcelona. The etched holes, lines, dug marks Brassai photographed & shared with the master who studied them, zeroing in on the naive, the primitive. Picasso compared them to his paper napkin animals. The day after he showed Brassai the white dog (of death) with cigarette-burn holes for eyes, word arrived of Nusch Eluard's passing.

The Good Dog

The city paid little attention to the lightning. Lightning hotter than the surface of the sun. Lightning, talk that changes things. Women all nonplussed. Men indifferent. Suddenly sauntering between two lines of cars a dog emerged from the Storrow Drive tunnel, immune from time, against the clogged artery. Haughty smile under his tongue. Baudelaire in his last prose poem praised the good dogs of Paris, the poor dogs, the muddy dogs, exiled by all but the homeless, & women past their prime ignored by the imbecility of men. This outlaw mutt, shaggy, wet, yet getting somewhere faster than the rest of the rush-hour commuters. Unleashed grin of freedom, progress in its own way.

Precedents

for **Rohan Nunes**

There are precedents for what you do, carrying gifts of coffee & breadfruit out of Jamaica, following that star to more northern climes. I stood under the sun at Solstice thinking of you up in Stockholm for the midnight sun on your twenty-first birthday. I imagined you one of the Magi kings. Dig this, Rohan! In 1960 Miles & Coltrane played in that Scandinavian capital. For some jazz fans, perhaps, the first Black men they ever saw. They played "All Blues" that night, for you.

Under the Spell of the Ballerina

I worked up a good sweat walking cross town from the MFA to North Station, when a gust of air rushed down the outdoor corridor. Fresh at first, like an Atlantic, amniotic memory, in the distance guys in hard hats emerged from the tunnel, along with the smell of refuse, blood, the dead. I continued on under the spell of Degas' ballerina with crossed arms, her Zen elbows at rest, & Walter Benjamin's fascination with the ability of objects to withstand the gaze. At home the low, gentle timbre of your voice fleshed out the next second, to the full.

New Moon

Sharp new moon carves its way above tenements in the blue afternoon. Difficult to hold to thoughts of luck, or justice, or even beauty, when tunneling through icy December air the grey-haired Asian woman rolls a steel cart piled with plastic bags of cans & bottles against the oncoming traffic. Suddenly the antithesis of such abstract concepts culminates in her hunchback, becoming their equal. How to come to love the shattered balance of breach of bone & cartilage? Today, I begin the struggle toward an aesthetics of obliquity, loss, & deformation. Rich, boffo, normalcy? Let the devil go ahead!

In the Arms of Two Black Shadows

The 7:00 A.M. ferry, *Nora Vittoria,* to Boston Harbor. Sun doing a slow, classical dance of pink-green light under tons of gray clouds. The rain all night moving off, east. A long way from the daily grind, & for a split second I was indigent on the beach in Martinique in the arms of two black shadows of palm trees. But then a fellow commuter in a three-piece suit dropped his briefcase next to me with a white, invasive thud.

The Only Open Ground

They're sifting for the remains of a 14-year-old girl in the only open ground left in Mattapan says the front page of the paper the woman seated across from me is giggling behind. She's fast forwarded to the comics. When she coughs she doesn't cover her mouth. The girl's father says she was a good girl. She didn't deserve to get punched in the stomach, stabbed, shot. She was pregnant, after all.

Dream Naked

The day before she appeared as archetypally as the snake goddess of Crete, I had to remove the Christmas tree by taking it to a church, where if I dragged it down the aisle, (as I had in the vestibule) it would have left a mark. I picked it up in my arms, top bent as if it were the neck of a man, & turned around to find benches filled with trees covered with white cloths. Souls. Before me, near the altar, a line of about twenty people carrying trees the same way. We all waited for the blessing I could see going on up ahead, vestments, sacred movements, smoke of frankincense?

I woke, tossed the tree in the back of the truck, rigid, as if it were the real body - of a dead man - tossed upon a bier. When I got to the dump the trees at the top of the pile were covered with the white cloth (an Alba) of snow.

She appeared the morning of the seventeenth of January, Two Thousand, presenting two identical swords, red scabbards, gold hilts. One hers, the other soon mine. She pointed to framed paintings, photos on the wall, "Do you have the image of the mountain?" "Yes," I answered, "internally." We kissed, ceremoniously. She commented that I remained distant. It wasn't until I woke that I saw words in swords.

Wanting to Speak

It's written in Arabic. Hand-written script in two strips taped in my notebook. The translation is this: "I saw her & wanted to speak. But did not."

Discourse & Dialogue

The most anti-Socratic day in the history of the café. First person pronoun repeated so often it sounds as though everyone has an impediment. &, of course, as if on Narcissistic faith alone the whole cast of characters, whole life stories orchestrated alone, no questions asked. Look, listen, a few have solved all the problems of discourse & dialogue: all talking at the same time.

Am I Ever More Ecstatic?

> *...there's a street like Lyric Energy...*
> **-Max Jacob**

Am I ever more ecstatic than imagining the walk from Boulevard Raspail to rue du Vieux-Colombier with the awkward spires of St. Sulpice coming into focus, overhearing Walter Benjamin overhearing Adrienne Monnier, in 1930, talking with Leon-Paul Fargue regarding the incomparable nature of the neighborhood, & knowing Man Ray's experimental film, *Emak Bakia*, premiered on this street in 1926 before an audience of fifty people, Django on the soundtrack, as if in the back row, fingering the guitar lesson?

The Confusion

I did everything wrong before I could do one thing right. The Labor Day throng at North Station lined up congesting the rush-hour commute. Among the faceless mass, one fourteen-year-old, just under my daughter's age, strolled through the terminal accompanied by her peers. Regal, ethnic, Latin, Greek, dark, pure, sensual, all eyes upon her. She didn't turn her head to acknowledge the gaze, but stored it internally where it glowed, a nuclear core. I turned into an ancient pillar without salt, enlarging the foyer's space.

Her friends, maids, inferiors buying trinkets as if on a spree of freedom for the first time. She had everything she needed. Her skirt more than her parents could afford. Breasts hiked up & pushed a few years beyond her years. Her lack of modesty, the exact opposite of the Indian girl in the crowded Oaxacan market, almost invisible under the awning just down from the chocolate stalls, who turned my head so quickly Manuel Avila Camacho whispered, "Virgin!" which warned, "Do not touch, *even with your eyes!*"

I saw her heading in the opposite direction in Boston, not a care in the world, just one friend by her side. She & her entourage returned just in time to miss the Lowell train pulling out on track 10.

Again, she was unaffected. Plunked herself down on the floor, where the others followed suit nudging against her, & the near wall. It wasn't long before an old man barged his way on stage where the curtain of her skirt had just risen. He was the first person she responded to, the only one of the four to get out of the way of the white cane searching for its 90 degree truth, its familiar tapping on the floor to wall, wall to floor, finding only the confusion of human flesh.

Not hers. The others stubbornly stayed put. She peered into the blind man's glasses to see if there were a chance of fraud. For a second I felt more sorry for him than for any handicapped against the world - for what he'd missed!

He made it through the last gate which opened automatically. She left immediately with her knapsack, came back changed into a pair of casual shorts & nondescript top, merging her more with the others her own age.

In retrospect, I see the old man's celestial train ascend, & wonder who, if anyone else, noticed her at all.

Dancer/Danger

Seven yellow & black plastic cones stand guard on the sidewalk in front of Philip Johnson's chess-set "King & Queen," International Place. I read *dancer* in misprision. Of course, it's *danger people / working above*. I don't dare look up until crossing High St. From this vantage I see the staged platform strung by joists & cables at the top floor. What more can they want, those jettisoned souls in the wind, than vertiginous reach, squeegee, harness, stone-winged temerity?

Minutiae: Audience for the Dance

Or the time I brought her to see, *Minutiae,* before she knew it as part of a stage set for a dance Rauschenberg constructed on the wing in 48 hours. "I would love to take my clothes off behind there!"

Noticing the lace on the lower panel, "The lace, also, makes me want to take my clothes off!"

She's the archaic red figure dripping, bled on the blue of the largest screen. Before the black orb (mirror) suspended in space cut out of the front panel, "It is the eye, the seeing eye, the visionary eye seeing through the piece, which also makes me want to take my clothes off!"

Is it any wonder that of all the works in this artist's vast repertoire, this is the one I'd choose?

Confessional Poem

Something ended up taking your place in bed, almost haphazardly, while you were in California. My notebooks.

Our Portable Abode

Walked a good hour into the forest until no footprints appeared on the overnight snow along the path. Warmer toward the interior. You planned where you might survive the night. Pine boughs balanced snow as if they blossomed. According to the compass we'd catch sight of ocean at high ground continuing due east. Space unearthed an inaudible din. Language pitched our portable abode.

One Day in the Same Vicinity

December second chill causing one face to stand out from the rest in the line for the bus on Huntington Avenue. Sure, everyone wants to get a seat, all want to beat the imminent rush hour, but for this guy, last in line, an entire felt blanket folded & draped around his neck, dread in his eyes, night's the real concern. The sun that's left, sharp angle out of the northwest, is still of value. No more sunsets from this vantage in the city anymore. It's light, then not. Survivable day, night's threat. Suddenly the image of the fetish sled hauling folded felt & fat props itself up between him & me, & I realize the whole of Beuys's marrow bone of art. Though this guy wouldn't get it, he's closer to it.

II
The little square's deserted as the temperature turns cold, & wind ignores Canada's borders. He's not there now, but in warmer weather I'd catch Dakar sitting on the bench, exactly as he was as magistrate in Ghana, formerly The Gold Coast. I asked him once to tell me his most notorious cases. Seems a minister siphoned off parishioner funds. Brought in by members of his church, Dakar chastised him sharply, gave him probation, & a chance to pay it back, in installments. On the other hand, a woman was found with stolen jugs of beer hidden in the rafters of her house. Pregnant, she couldn't have done it by herself, but wouldn't reveal who else helped. She spent a year in jail, for which the judge claimed no regrets. Slowly, though, I sensed a deep discomfort, covered by calm demeanor, finally reaching bone-chilling, sinewy, ill at ease.

At the Foot of Wall Street, 1998

They're serving excellent rations at the front in the war on Wall St. It's reported brokers & bankers prefer thick red meat. An elite corps of French wines, Chateau Margaux, 1900, knocked down by their big guns, $10,000 a bottle at Patroon. The battle frenzy is hard to fathom. I read that Iraqi children are too malnourished to play with each other. It makes them too sad to think about their dead friends. Over sixty years ago in the middle of the Depression Berenice Abbott turned her camera on the foot of Wall St. The Whitehall Building remained formidable. Seaplanes at the Downtown Skyport, grounded. There in the foreground of the shot, the two young, unsmiling shoeshine boys. She got it all down in black & white, the spilled blood of childhood.

Pail for Ganymede

I'm walking down Fulton Street doing my best to manage the difficulty, (staying in the moment), toward the end of a century whose harshness is matched only by its portent: a turn for the worse.

Two lead faucets lie dead in the street from the renovations going on at #140. Picking them up, suddenly the Sun is Rembrandt's Zeus disguised as an eagle lifting the woefully, uncoddled Ganymede, (Look, the kid's pissing himself, & the grapes are falling from the cluster onto the last he'll see of that ground), to Olympus!

The solid weight of the faucets, out of the height of the Machine Age, balance each other like the Twin Towers over my shoulder.

    *   *   *   *

Written after a walk with my wife & daughters from our rooms at the Algonquin Hotel down Broadway to the Seaport in 1992, & based on the Rauschenberg Combine by the same title.

Lithe

When I met, talked to, shook hands with Judith Jamison on 7th St. in Washington, she danced before, around, & through me, standing still.

Great Vehicle Body

Great vehicle body, unmatched by Lamborghini, French TGV, Cunard, NASA. Seal on the ice floe just beyond Spectacle Island in Boston Harbor.

Dream & Intoxication

for **Joe Schuyler**

Pushed so hard against the wall, I passed through, or the door swung open. Gathering stones for my wife's garden, you, your name, face & graceful movement rose up. When I draped 80 lbs. of topsoil over my shoulder, as one might adjust a man just down from the cross, it jolted recollection of the dream the week before, picturing you recumbent under a shroud, or sheet, supine with Mantegna's experimental view of the divine body. Unlike that image, you stirred. To my great relief, the crypt turned quickly to bed.

Remember that night at the jazz club on Bleecker? *Boomer's* opened ten years before the *Blue Note*. We got there early. Just us, & two dressed-alike lesbians, who swam around in the dark in response to the uncanny angles of your camera. Posing this way, that, pouting, preening, purring, prevailing. One grand voyeuristic experience, even if I called my own part non-involvement at the time. How long passed before anyone else showed up?

Cedar Walton played there that year, but that night a group of unknowns blew us away. Dream & intoxication, Nietzsche claimed *the* two sources of art, & that only the artist can settle into the abyss between them. Young nymphs you caught on film. Horn section. Polyphonic percussion. Wine, whiskey, the 3 A.M. dithyrambic trek back home to 14th Street.

Coming to, the next morning, standing on the sidewalk in front of your apartment, waiting for you to join me for coffee, a woman with a small dog turned around toward me, & in a familiar tone said, "Screw?"

Trying briefly to decipher the message, "Excuse me?" "*Screw Magazine,* didn't I see you in the offices of *Screw?*"

Then flew down 14th Street between dream & intoxication.

It's Obvious

Across the room of the dream the guy in anger, whiskey bottle in hand, dropped his vicious stare, momentarily, then sat down next to me. "It's obvious," he complained, "that you are protected by women & books."

With Additional Light

> *Charrette: the working out of a difficult architectural problem.*

Tired of leaving every morning in the dark, I slept in a little bit. When I woke she was carrying the window's tactile light around the bedroom on her skin. I hadn't seen her getting dressed for work in months. When she opened the drawer burgeoning with underthings there was a veritable explosion of color, but that was dead paper & spent gunpowder compared to the white pair of panties & beige bra she put on.

I let her go off on her daily, circuitous route like the moon, admired, but untouched. I'm familiar with the scourge of excessive desire. I took a leisurely pace to work. A few blocks away one of my Cape Verdean neighbors in a purple shirt & copper straw hat added mortar to a cinderblock retaining wall. A fledgling heron floated over the local pond as if summer were the only season to contend with.

At 8:35, admiring the lion heads alternating just above each modillion supporting the cornice of the present Charrette, I caught sight of a Peregrine falcon, rapid-fire wing thrusts in contrast to the usual gull. It lives in the Custom House tower. I wonder when its day is done? When it can return home like a hieroglyph to an obelisk?

This Vanishing Architecture

On the afternoon of the solstice, sun wedged down an alley at the lower end of Water St. where bright wrought iron lines of fire escapes burned blacker shadows against fading white brick. Water St. is all business now, but those extended rows of metal give evidence of its former, teeming tenement life. I saw the walls as sheet music. Hustle & bustle of immigrant voices, noise, once imprisoned in this vanishing architecture, let out!

Prestige, from the French: Illusion, Trick, to Blind

A German investment group purchased One Liberty Square, just one in a series of architectural gems realtors term "Jewel Boxes." The others are 176 Federal, One Winthrop Square, 85 State, & 45 Milk. The latter is now on the market. The other day I overheard an agent from Trammel Crow steer two clients' gaze away from that building, pitching the prestige of proximity to Ben Franklin's birthplace, a few doors down. When they weren't looking the serpents of the caducei carved on all 16 columns of the sale property slid from their winged staffs, & turned the box of jewels into a sarcophagus of bones & dust.

The Little Band

If I could begin with the way summer exacts deeper shadows from trees, or the amethyst depths of the waters Proust used to frame his little band of girls led by Albertine at Balbec, I would, but the subway grows no trees, provides no glimpse of seas. My girls are sad on Monday, the one with pigtails down the small of her back can't lift her head, while her friend with the guitar case serenades her with a chorus of questions, she responds only with nods & shakes. Two days later her pallor turns carefree. She's gulping down sugar-coated cereal from the box, & expounding on topics from world affairs to boys.

How about the time they stared at the Nike ad of the aborigine wearing a python over his shoulders down torso to knees? "Why is he naked?" her own breasts barely there, & hair free flowing as if never cut. The little musician shrugged no answer, but stared hypnotic at the snake where the genitals hid. What, a month left until school gets out? I'm going to miss this duo, their get-ups, prancing, pouts, lipstick hearts drawn on cheeks. My own little band will soon be off for the summer with their sneakers cut off at the toe, their inquisitiveness, & haloes, until next year when they'll probably take a different train to maturity, & the temporary hell of high school.

Music of Venice

> *One might sit at the piano for fifty years, trying out all possible combinations of notes, & still never come up with a phrase as divine as a great musician.*
> **- Proust**

All week I desired to know the music of Venice, listening to Vespers, examining the impact of the architecture of St. Mark's on the choral dynamics of the Gabrielis. On the morning after a black storm, lightning close, vivid, visceral, I dreamt of sitting at an outdoor table, the water to my left, the waiter taking away dishes & glasses, talking. I told him to listen. I ordered seconds of lemon sole & Sancerre. The dream light matched the flesh of Venice. A woman strolling by turned & smiled. I recognized her. Past love. Illicit love. She sat down, arm around me. Then I realized our chair was a piano bench filled with sheets of music, the dream's redemptive gesture, an internal orchestration.

The Duality

You'll find the neighbor's wife quite congenial, unable to pass up a chance to wave, shout hello, comment on whatever you're doing at the time. Industrious, too. Five children running around the yard, & another with her own kid who visits often, she still has time to tend the flowers, water, weed. All done in an array of flowing dresses, red, green, & her favorite see-through yellow. He's Sicilian. She's from the north in blood & physiognomy. I half expect her one day, while the old man's on another 12-hour shift operating heavy machinery at the Big Dig, to sit out there on the back stairs with her recruited daughter revealing the same profiles as Carpaccio's *Two Courtesans*, (the painting Marcel gave Albertine as an example of the duality of women's faces, the one we see, & the one below) each frozen in summertime.

Her Secret Recipe

> *One could see its red-tiled floor gleaming like porphyry. It seemed not so much the cave of Francoise as a little temple of Venus…*
>
> **- Proust**

One moment she's headed to San Diego for a conference, the next, she & I are headed down the Grand Canal, suddenly docking at St. Mark's. The young Venetian sailor turned around to say that she was his. What with this a dream, sure, we believed it, & broke apart. The sky held firm. The damned boat, no gondola, but a two-hundred-ton barque. I grabbed the guy by the T-shirt saying, "Look, I know I haven't fought for her, but I will!"

Still believing this specter of my wholly Proustian jealously, I leapt overboard planning to return. Must have thought I could swim, jumping starboard.

I could hear her crying as I ran down the canal, shoes plashing off the dirty green liquid as if it were a puddle. What was I more enthralled with, her cry, or my new-found talent? I climbed up at the first convergence of the next canal. Saw two stone alcoves where bread rose on tables under different cloths. An old woman kneaded the dough inside the cloth tied in knots, over & over, in open spaces between the knots, waiting patiently to let it rise. Her secret recipe, her metaphor for Love.

The Little Phrase

I remember a long work week, feeling the relief of Friday. Dusk draped everything in heavy light. I noted the swabbies on a wooden raft washing the outside of the luxury liner, *Odyssey*, down to a plate-clean blue. The *Amethyst Kriti* headed out after emptying its hold of oil. A ton of activity in Boston Harbor. Then a miraculous image. I'm sure no one on the ferry noticed, but me. At the far end of the parking lot next to the Federal Courthouse a white rectangle placed on the black bumper of the red cab of a huge crane turned out to be a sheet of music with the akimbo slant of the limbs of the violinist standing to the side, playing. Although I heard nothing but the engines' groan, it was as if the little phrase of the Vinteuil sonata, which the reader never really gets to hear in Proust, floated across the water as a color, as a tactile vibration, soundlessness only an alerted skin could interpret, & turn the inaudible body language into music.

The Present is the Roof of Time

Just when morning fog prevents changes of light against the walls, causes this waterfront architecture to remain static, at the top of Milk St. in front of the Old South Meeting House one of the foreign flower girls performs an ancient ritual, a re-enactment of the beauty once found, & immortalized by so many Greek sculptors & architects. Tall, she moves with ease, elbows even with her shoulders balancing flattened cardboard boxes that an hour before, millennia before, contained gladioli, irises, strawberries, oranges, roses, yes, a living caryatid, the long bodily architectonic column of Time.

IV. from *The Book of Assassinations*

Let no thought pass incognito, and keep your notebook as strictly as the authorities keep their register of aliens. - **Walter Benjamin**

The tendency to draw a moral from the situations encountered in a modern city is characteristic of Baudelaire, and is what gives his prose poems in particular their unique blend of observation and commentary, the sense that the most random of events offers itself to interpretation. - **Rosemary Lloyd**

I believe that in many cases, though certainly not all, Poe's inebriation was mnemonic, a method of work, an energetic and deadly method, but one suited to his passionate nature. The poet had learned to drink as a careful writer fills notebooks with observations. - **Baudelaire**

One might go so far as to say that the sky — in Baudelaire — is made of language and it is this celestial language that gives time, memory, and perception to man. - **Elissa Marder**

Always be a poet, even in prose. - **Baudelaire**

The Woman & the Lotus

She is leafing through a book in the library with all the nonchalance of a rubber tree brushed by a steady wind in a valley in Vietnam. With the lilting half-syllables of someone who has to pick up the language at fourteen, she turns & says, "Robert, you know, in my country," pointing to a photograph in the book on waterlilies, "this is the lotus, & my grandfather would put tea in the flower, leave it overnight while it closed, & gather it again in the morning. It smells *so* good."

I watched her eyes reach back through that Proustian sensation to childhood. Now, she's a senior majoring in chemical engineering. "&, you know, Robert, my people would feed the horse the tea, then kill the horse. They take it out of the stomach in a few days. It was very expensive."

Lan told me once that her name means "orchid." Another time, after I showed her some pieces I'd written about my wife, & other women observed on the street, Lan paused, & in her way, intoned, "This weekend I must go shopping… to make more poems… *for the world!*"

One Day, Discrete

The day's wandering around aimlessly. It doesn't want to be on the calendar. Doesn't rebel against the slightest breeze, but goes right along with it, without second guessing, not questioning a thing. O.K., it may cringe a little at the innocuous noise of all the lawnmowers, may even be grateful for the bevy of dragonflies patrolling the skies, but it seems fed up with tragedy. Doesn't want the Monday *Times*! Resisting dates, ignoring wars, it wants no part of history! Wants to be left alone.

Told This Way

He told it this way: When the car reminded him of the mechanical facts of truth, by not starting, by granting him perhaps more time than he wanted there, having already decided to pick up & head home, but with the lesson evident inside the battery, the alternator, he opened one of the books in his bag to a page marked by an old photo of himself. He was young. Skin fair, smooth. As thin, he said, as he'd ever been. The shot taken, posed. Standing, reading one of the French poets. But while he waited for the tow truck, with more time than he really wanted to ponder it, what struck him was how much he must not have known back then. How, if someone were to take a similar shot now, the same would hold true. Yet, what he also saw emanating from the early, "literary" portrait was the added factor, (apparent in evanescent circles of doubt surrounding the eyes,) of *realizing then* just how much he didn't know. Giving him hope that that same humility might now carry him through.

My Violent American Way of Handling Things

A snow drift. Your hip. Early sun off the frozen sea. A week ago they forbade my writing at work, exiling me, a lovesick Ovid at Tomi. But yesterday as I disembarked, Scott, one of the sailors on the *Nora Vittoria*, reminded me that today would be Valentine's, & that I should make sure I "get something for Kathleen." So today I board the later, slower *Matthew J. Hughes* to do just that, fetch the burgeoning language. At the moment, the sun at stern, David's latest postcard, a Tapies collage sent from Barcelona marking the page I was reading when Scott thought of you, I finish the page referring to Place des Vosges & rue de Rennes, reminding me of the night we entertained two neighborhood ladies headed to Paris in less than a month. We brought out Chablis from the cellar, the Gewürztraminer from the fridge, I baked the sole, you served pastries from the French shop in Cohasset. As much as I talked about our favorite restaurant on narrow Bertin-Poiree running down from Rivoli to Quay Megisserie & the Seine, as much recommending Musee d'Orsay & Carnevalet in order to avoid the lines surrounding the Louvre, the shops along rue de Buci, even St. Sulpice over Notre Dame, (although I flashed to the time we sat outside Baudelaire's apartment at Hotel Lauzun with a little picnic, when the young clochard crawled out from under the Pont Marie heading toward us like a large grey rat forcing me to show the glint of the blade of my Swiss Army knife his way in the sun turning him right around, forcing me to feel guilty for my violent American way of handling things,) more than recommending the festival atmosphere of *La Coupole* to them, or warning them away from a day trip to the cliché of Fontainebleau, well, during the whole night's jovial conversation what struck me most was the undercurrent of their loneliness. Their husbands long gone. So I pit that absence against our togetherness, knowing that there'll be a time when memories of Paris, the gorgeous windows along rue de Rennes, will be all that's left, memory itself representing absence as opposed to the snow drift this morning, or the immediacy of the skin of your hip. The *Hughes* just docked. I'll type this up tonight, exiled from nothing.

Choreography of Desire

Because it was present, streaming steadily, swirled, & landed with the nuance of dance, dream snow proved equal to real snow.

How Much More Alive Can a Man Be?

One of those mundane Mondays when one might as well be interred, or disinterred, for that matter. Everything so familiar, nothing stands out. Then Claire writes from Pittsburgh that stone heads above Roman doors convey welcome & demarcation; David wonders from London if I've seen the Medusas placed sideways to avoid the Pagan evil eye in the basilica cistern in Istanbul; & by pure chance, a couple of hours later, Itir writes from her cousin's house on the Asian side of the city that I wouldn't believe the voluptuousness of the Virgin Tower in the middle of the Bosporus, while watching sunset on the European side of Istanbul. Suddenly I'm lifted up, risen by tension carved in stone in Rome, & by the generous hand that wrote it. Far, far from immune to the power of the evil eye, poets are able to avert that gaze by inversion of ego toward creativity, & the love of the language of fellow men. How much more alive can a man be, when out of the mundane of every day, a Virgin surfaces out of narrow straits linking Black & Mamara Seas, illuminated by a Byzantine-neon light, & quiet, humble tongue?

Keeping the First Heat of Summer Cool

At some invisible juncture, I'm not sure of the name of the square, High St. changes into Summer. I know Lincoln St. shunts off to the left. Then past the pedestrian walkway of Washington St., up little Winter with all its record & shoe stores, which they often block off for Hip Hop, crossing Tremont to the Common, where Tony is banging out his "Junk Jam' on refrigerator vegetable & fruit bin drawers, stove grates, the usual plastic buckets, a lone bent-to-hell cymbal, a couple of sticks of wood, certainly no drumsticks, & two or three hubcaps for that high-pitched Caribbean steel-drum effect he likes to include every so often in the more than triple-beat African percussion he's got going, what with his ability to strike the bottom & the top of the rectangular refrigerator drawers almost simultaneously elevating it past the primitive toward a level of true American jazz, to the extent that a tall, obviously African young man comes over & stands close behind him, in awe really under his black umbrella keeping the first heat of summer off, trying to figure out just how Tony's "Junk Jam" operates. A big crowd of kids jumpin' & plunkin' down dollars their parents let them contribute, adults bopping, I'm smiling trying to keep from moving my white pugilistic moves, when a woman strikes up a conversation attesting to Tony's brilliance, even coughing up a sawbuck for his coverless CD, she's a writer who's written a book on forgiveness called "The Mystery of Forgiveness." Still really a doctoral dissertation, but I can tell Ruth Henderson is someone who knows all about forgiveness as it emanates & spreads, radiates really contagious like the jazz. Keep an eye out for her, the little blonde with the baseball cap, enormous presence. The last time I saw her she was talking to a young magician standing behind an infallible House of Cards, which might have been glued together. The last time I saw Tony he was counting out more money that I ever made from writing.

Music

I know some gentle people. Quiet places. I want to conjure words of solace, drown out cacophony of retribution, self-righteousness. Fog, help me today, mist, bare trees, any phone call from loved ones, family, friends, or email missives from colleagues concerned with art, the written word, music, color, blood running through veins burning for life. Smother the noise of Oedipal wrath. Seriously, meditatively, let's help each other turn away from gnashing teeth out of the West Wing. At the moment, I'm choosing one image. It's quite simple, & divine. It's eight-&-a-half-inches high from the island of Keros in the Cyclades. Harp player. A seated figure whose head tilts toward the sky in such a way that makes us wonder if he's blind. Long before Homer. Instrument decorated with bird's bills. Birds teaching man to sing? The simplicity of line is fascinating. How the sculptor carved him into this ceremonial throne, we'll never know. (My wife, & Maureen, & Alice just wrote. Words of love & encouragement. What courage means from Women!) Our blind musician's feet squarely on the ground. His hands are gone, no longer needs them, forever playing everything by ear, he's a funerary object placed in the grave to accompany the recently deceased in life beyond.

Large Tapestry

I don't need to tell you just how subtly spectacular sun is filtering through fog, a gauze, lace, tapestry, but there you have it, a reminder that that rarity still occurs on occasion, as it did when you were a kid, sequestering you, giving hints of your own individuality, if not immortality, when you didn't want it to lift the curtain of the stage of the fantastic world wanting to return to the quotidian. No, you soaked it all in as instantaneous as memory. The herd of wild horses stampeded off the neighbor's garage roof sounding more like birds than horses then must have wings.

Grotesque: Half Bird Half Man with an Infant's Foot & Elephant's Hoof

I stepped out the door a dove. Totally totemistic. The other birds greeted me, but let me be, half man half dove. The starlings all stayed together. The day, which looked overcast from indoors, had great open spaces where the sun overwhelmed roads, trees, ocean. I walked on the seawall with a feeling of utter exhilaration, you might say, flight. Stone outcroppings reminded me of the dream the night before when I was afraid to dive into the water, afraid one of the seals might bite me. Nevertheless I risked diving in in the dream, & now all fear vanished. At some point along the seawall a young girl walked through a fissure with the gait of an angel. When she turned round to see the half bird half man one of my feet turned into an elephant's hoof, the other into an infant's foot. Oh, did I hobble on that wall, but my totemistic bird wings propped me up. I was as normal as the eventuality of death.

The angel smiled. The sea smiled, in fact it laughed, at having now seen everything. Back when I was just a man, when reality was my only concern, I worked as a research librarian. I spent three long months going through archival boxes of Hemingway material at the JFK Library in Boston. I never found anything anyone else hadn't seen hundreds of times before, until one day in a letter to his publisher commenting on the celebration of his 50th birthday, a label from a wine bottle was glued to the third & last page of the handwritten letter. Against all laws I peeled back the 1937 Gevrey-Chambertin, & there it was in his hand, barley legible, scratched in pencil, "It's harder to live than die." I don't know why, after all these years have passed since finding the fragment, at this moment, half bird half man with an infant's foot & elephant's hoof, I realized the enormity of it. At the time I simply returned it to the page with a little saliva on my finger, determined to let him keep his secret.

The Play on the Body

It's ravishing opening the big side door of the hotel, window curtain swept up like an invisible dancer's dress. Ravishing, falling into dream, the naked dream. Ravishing the sun not quite up, delayed you might say below the horizon of clouds, sending up red to blue & pink. Ravishing to read the recently found fragment dug up in a small village library southwest of the Chang River in China. Attributed to Li Po, supposedly written under the influence of wine, "The Beauty of your Being & Mind, Intuition, Perception, Creativity, [etc., some lost, torn], will carry you far beyond the Force of your Physicality. Vessel containing the Rest." Scholars say the play on body & terra-cotta pottery is obvious, what with the latter's 8,000 year history refined at the height of the Tang & the poet. The clay's firing reminds one of lightning, which Fenollosa called the sentence, or the sudden spark flying off the body of a dancer in a move rarely seen before.

Documents: Homage to the Body

...the naked truth within naked death...
-Walter Benjamin

A Russian winter, one writer would call it here, where his "hair is very electric," so cold it freezes any trace of moisture, which is how I saw it this morning: cold shocking less than droplets into visible form, dried instantly to disappearance. What with the sun vivid as a virgin's lactating teat, a pure light show, air chilled to her bones. Damned birds darting around in delirium, knowing nothing other to do than fly! The heat in the house can't stoke up. I wear my scarf, bathrobe, wool blanket from Chiapas head to toe, & turn my back toward the sun through picture window. My other writer just ordered tea & vodka in Moscow, saying, "Warmth turns fleeting time itself into a drink of ecstasy." A third cup of coffee. Ankle tendons taut as snowshoe strings trekking across tundra. Benjamin helps Asja Lacis into her galoshes. My wife gone for five days now, I've begun to love the cold. It's no surprise to learn he loves Asja's flaws, wrinkles, moles, tawdry clothes. Stay out of this for another second, California, come in quiet & clear, Gorky Street: death lets love live, as sensate as skin, long after, in its own realm.

To a Red-haired Beggar Girl

Strange ending up in the little alcove of an urban academic library, where the claustrophobia of the reading room goes on unnoticed by five female students intent on projects & homework, psychology textbooks, computer printouts. The latest piercings around nostrils, tattoos at the smalls of backs just above elastic ridges of panties riding up over fashionable belts & jeans. Two skeletons, one hanging, the other stanchioned by a metal bar, populate a corner given over to the anatomy of Art. I want to attribute genders to them, too. More students arrive, & the librarian flashes concern at my leather bag & the copy of **Les Fleurs du Mal** I found in the stacks. Otherwise, unobtrusive, granting them their negligible presences equal to my own. All I can see now is Baudelaire's red-haired beggar girl in the alley of the kitchen door of the Paris bistro pleading silently for scraps, whose rags are riches caressing her nakedness.

History of Tragedy

I'm moving on, slowly, from my Greek mode. Stepping away from Homer, Herodotus, Seferis, Elytis, & now, Cavafy. But not without a final reference, a goodbye. I was out on the deck of the *Nora Vittoria*, not the usual side, I got there late & had to settle for the less crowded, unsunny side. I'm telling you, there was a monologue of a conversation in progress that almost killed me. She went on & on. The two listeners were prisoners. I had to bear to overhear the tone, excruciating, babbling, mindless. Caught only fragments, & the tone, repeated first person pronoun, & constant references to "all my friends, my best friend," etc. The captive audience's reaction was telling. "You went through all that for that?" I couldn't help it. I yelled into the wind, "Come up for air! What a saga! A real sea story!" I don't know where my words went. But hers intruded on the unsunny side of my being, just as I was trying to read Cavafy.

Docking, I moved away from them into the light. Reading his "Ancient Tragedy," in the light, away from her inane noise. His praise of the great dramatists, no need to mention them, & their characters, the ones who fought death to the death. I loved so much the retrieval of Alcestis from the realm of the dead by Heracles, who arrived upon the scene at an opportune moment! Cavafy's poem purged the evil American spirit of meaninglessness soiling my head. I needed this ancient reminder, when later that morning I read in the newspapers the postmodern reenactment of Tragedy by ancient characters in Srebrenica. Over a hundred buses, like Roman *deus ex machina*, delivering mourners to the site where 8,000 were killed seven years before.

On stage: Alija Camdzic & his wife Hava, who lost two sons, a pregnant daughter-in-law, & a five-year-old granddaughter in the largest massacre [in Europe] since WWII. **His lines**: "I have lost everything a man can lose. But that's not the biggest tragedy. The biggest tragedy is that I'm still alive." **Enter**: Mujo Berberovic, who seven years ago, fleeing Serb Army forces through the forest with his wife, Mina, & their five-year-old son, Aldin, knowing the enemy searched to kill men of fighting age, decided to separate from them. **His lines**: "What a mistake that was. I keep cursing the day we separated. If I could have just a cup of coffee with my Mina. Just once."

Émigrés

Well past the dog days of August into what must be quiet cat days. No barking at all in early afternoon. The poplar leaves looking like bells, but silent. It's a time that goes unnoticed except by émigrés, poets, the eternal longing of the dead to hear more than they do now, the barely audible purr.

Far Worse than This Deadening Cold

A deadening cold even black coffee can't thaw. Four above. Ducking inside *Borders Café* on Washington Street the meager group of early-morning *literati derelicti* remind me of last night's dream: in the supermarket looking for artichoke hearts, some woman offers a package of celery hearts, which I reject; two thugs' vicious stares; a pair of illegal, fifteen & a half year olds, flirting, whom I barely avoid; & finally, the woman with a dog climbing the magazine rack, asking her what kind it is, she says, "Rat catcher," whose tail, as it slinks past me, is fox's, my friend the fox, sniffing out thugs.

What I feared most this morning, what with a clean-bill of health from the doctor on Monday relieving me from months' fearing the worst, was the trek up Milk Street. I mentioned Milk this summer when heat was so oppressive one looked forward to a day like this. Wednesday's wind is visible shaking windows to foundations. Still find Time enough to stop, peer through scarf long enough to read the small plaque on the tree in Post Office Square Park: "Aristocratic Pear." The one with a recently sawn-off limb just above its trunk. The only aristocratic amputee I've known, Blaise Cendrars, knew Siberian winter, Rio & Cannes in summer. A poet who could exact rhythm out of blood, earth, sea, & far worse than this deadening cold, the marrow pain beyond his missing limb.

That Face

The cops won't let Eddie sell papers at the State Street subway stop for the store down on Washington. At his age he'll never bother getting a vendor's license. Told me he visited his wife for two years in the nursing home before taking her back for the final six months, bathing her twice a day. Wishes he bought a second black leather jacket like the one he wears for $10 long ago. Worked at Suffolk Downs for years, with betting slips, not the horses. Selling papers on the sly is as close to begging as a man can get. Today Eddie had his blue duffel bag, one paper out, hiding like a criminal at the back entrance. Still has regulars who give him a *finnif*, not for the paper, (they don't read the *Herald*,) but for that face he's mastered, lugubrious, a word straight out of hard-scrabble, ancient Sicily with roots in doleful & mournful, especially to a ludicrous degree. One could call Eddie an artist, a mime, more than con.

As Quiet as One Can Get

White shirt & sunglasses in the sun. The blue sand below: years of pulverized mussel shells. The big, old oil tanker, *Saraband*, pushed through the Hull channel Gut by a Boston tug. All the quarried granite shoring up the land. A whole wall of morning glories & unidentified grasses. Black shadows opening the eyes of stones.

Moment in Monument

Desire underlies form. For two days running I delay my trek to work detouring into the mammoth bookstore chain. Read the fine Polish poet who flies on the wings of memory back to a cold & rainy adolescence surrounded by twisted Communist tongues he now straightens, retranslating the past into legible language, calling up dead mentors, sister, Warsaw, Lvov. A shaft of light from one of the high windows of this building helps me try to stand against his practice, in the presence of my own desire, however dissatisfied. Hard as I try though thoughts of my first wife's grandfather filter through repression. "Judgu, sure I'll join you for a whiskey." The lady I knew from the library who said she'd bring me something back from the shrine of the Black Madonna at Czestochowa. Where is that medal like a memory?

I favored presence. Went off to work hypersensitive to scents, fuel exhaust, bread baking, faces, actions, minor stillnesses I tried to compare to waning trumpet chords sliding down Venetian walls at St. Mark's, obviously without success. The voice of the black man warning me my briefcase was open as I rode the escalator from the subway writing this was far more appropriate, more immediate. Then the undeniable. Dream undeniable desire. Past as desire. That night I rode in the boat heading back to the bridge trestle we'd seen young men dive from, like the other time I saw them in the dream diving through the other side of Time. Ahead of us they swam. We swam with them toward the trestle, the young men, then, surprised, *my first wife*, & I.

Most of us naked. She looks so young! The young men love her visage! It's getting crowded, bodies bumping, funneling like fish toward the trestle, where a spokesman stands on land saying we have to wait to get permission from the State to climb the wooden beams. I feel old electrical cords tied to underwater pilings press against my skin. Lose sight of her. Make it to the small spit of land where the director, or commissar, says that in the Meantime a theatre company will stage some Gorkyesque lower depths. I crouch covering my genitals. Cold & scared. Then like a miracle she approaches, smiling, dressed in the layered gold & purple garb of her Polish ancestry. Gently, she bends down toward my shamed nakedness surrounded by actors, audience, sea, fully clothed in truth, she whispers through cupped hand next to my ear, "You can't call a taxi."

About American Poetry

More interested in finding than knowing. The symposia throng, led by panels, almost political, mostly American, addressing the question, "What is American about American poetry?" Attending both sessions separately, one at JFK Center for The Performing Arts, the next a week later, at The Library of Congress. Time-warped opinions of panelists quoting Frost, Dickinson & Stevens. They were against all projects, or series, the poem must be occasional, especially symbolic. Even mentioned Mallarmé. It took someone, an Irishman in the audience, Denis Donoghue, well into day two, to bring up Olson's name. Someone in the audience referred to painters' ability to be abstract, non-referential, so why not poetry? Hell no! Language must stand for something else, must symbolize with metaphor & simile. With dire trepidation I stood up to quote Olson's, "The trouble with the symbol is, it does not trouble." The entire panel turned a deaf ear, except a lone silent nod at the end of the table, the quick affirmation from the line of Gogol & Dostoevsky, the hoarse, smoker's nod from Joseph Brodsky.

Perhaps I Went a Little Too Far

A radical change in temperature, some 40 degrees between the two days, produced an unusual fog. In the midst of it, & Boston Harbor, the huge tanker, *Rio Blanco*, out of Valparaiso. Deck, white, hull, black. Its top half disappeared into the massive, purple mountain, seemingly right at home, as if it were Chilean landscape. When I dug down a little, researching what the geography of this boat, these sailors were heading back to in the next few weeks, perhaps I went a little too far, stumbling on Charles Darwin 168 years ago lying down in the woods in Talcahuano, south of Valparaiso, when the earth shook under him, & a great wave rose up, visible from a distance of four miles away. This man of science doesn't dust himself off, look up at the sky & give thanks he wasn't at the shore, where the tidal wave crashed at a height of 23 feet. No, he complains that the natives blame the wave on an old Indian woman who took credit for stopping the volcano on Antuco two years prior. Although he notes that they see the connection between suppression of the volcano & the quake, he can't forgive them, their lack of empiricism.

Another Key to the Dwelling

> ...*the occasion is the nothng that lets everything come forth.*
> **K.**

How much grey does it take to amount to blue? I'm always writing *the immediate-erotic,* in Kierkegaard's phrase, instinctual spark of the sensuous. In other words, always in love. To fall out of such a state is dangerous. Words won't come. The loss stops all sound, especially assaults music. So recently when the abyss opened, & love fell, a cellar-door key through a sewer grate: spelunk! I almost panicked.

She & I walked through the woods. An unfamiliar stand of pine, spruce, oak, eerie without a trace of wildlife. Absence of other species haunted our talk, our view, a foreboding we refused to let mar the pre-holiday mood. Figured it was probably the dogs apartment dwellers traipsed through with thinking they're doing nature a favor. A single nuthatch at the edge of the reservoir, fast enough to elude any predator, the lone exception.

Held hands & whispered love-making plans along the way. She would wear that 3-by-5-square-inch garment under a black skirt, green Christmas bra under nothing. The sensuous surrounded us like the genie who protects all innocent loves. Absence of fauna added a constant refrain of caution.

Returning to the beginning of the trail where the geologic period, & history of the area are posted, a guy drives up & gets out of an old white Monte Carlo saying do we know where Sheep's Head is? "What's that?" I ask.

Sheep's (Freudian stutter) Head, someplace I heards round here. Killer's eyes, & there's another guy in the passenger seat. "No," *fear-terror pause,* this is only our second time out here, don't know where it or much else is, already moving with her away by the arm toward silence.

He looks up pretending to study the map. I let her in. Shut the door. Look back to see him bobbing & weaving, peering into the mini-van he's parked in a handicapped space next to, & through the line of parked cars --- at us!

I back out. He backs out with quick-get-away-car handling. I drive away. Check, but do not catch him in the rear-view mirror: jailbird, murderer, marauder, the aura breathtaking breath taking breath...

Safe at home, I tell her I'll make the fire. Pour a glass of Port. I'll get the wood in the same jacket, with the National Geographic cap I had on in the parking lot, & turn from the wood pile to glimpse an early-model white vehicle drive by on the main drag in front of our rented duplex. Damned adrenaline mixing perception with paranoia. Stand behind bare lilac to see if they saw you. Get in the house, fool! Don't tell her. See if the car rides by. A car rides by. & again. Whispered plans of love-making ring echo hollow. Hello, she says, what's wrong? I tell her. Maybe, maybe not, as I check directory in case of emergency.

Night passes. New rules now in place. No unlocked cellar door. Outside lights on all night. Never, never walk in the woods where absence reigns.

The next morning I went out to start the car. She'd left the cellar door open for one of the kids who'd gone on an early morning jog without her key. I lose it. *The immediate-erotic,* & protection of the sensuous, disappear. I yell. She says if I have a heart attack & die it will be my own goddamn fault.

Could not write. Barely spoke. For three days. Though the next day I took her to the lake to see the heron, which the day before looked toward me, a great tuft of winter feathers with enough grey to amount to blue. It wasn't there for her, nor was I.

Tonight, after writing this, I'll bring some juice up to her in bed. She's fallen ill. I'll crawl in, silently, trying to approach her, as if nothing happened.

Distance & Absence

Waiting. Again, waiting. For her, again. For five days, clock, watch, enemies. Waiting, especially at night, cannot close the gaps of distance or absence. Distance: no real voice, cell phone be damned! Absence: no flesh. Until the last dawn is up: alone, waiting. Of course, one prefers to wait alone. At times, when both elements of waiting, distance & absence, so resemble death, it is as if one attends a funeral vigil. One stands, kneels, sits, lies down, waiting, akin to death.

Serving the Sentence

What happens to the world in four days & three nights without her is a transformation I'm forced into from the sultriness of her sprawled out naked on the bed napping with a linen sheet thrown partially over to keep the heat off in the afternoon readying for her trip to Salt Lake City with snow barely melting on its Icarean mountaintops. I stay quiet trying not to disturb her though my heart reaches out my hands don't & suddenly she's gone up & out West & the weather in the East changes radically with a rough fog riding in like a dusty cowboy. Damned Sun gets stubborn & halting political Refusnik in rumpled clothes of clouds forcing me into exile in-house staying up late confused dreaming awake under blankets we put away months ago so the wine disappears & the food gets scarce & mud starts oozing over the grass & roses threatening to cross the threshold over which I once carried her into Paradise where big catalpa & fig leaves burgeoned. Now recede into cactus thorns stuck in the back of my hand like fish hook barbs or the desolation of carpets like filthy streets I know in Veracruz, Belgrade, Venice, Chelsea, Memphis, Boston, but not Salt Lake City. The great teacher necessity turns me round & the aging process reverses stomach flattens teeth drop coffee stains into the imagined mud while I'm on all fours bellowing at the moon hidden in eclipse in touch with instinctual animal nature where solitude is more than an outward shadow but an internal reckoning without words.

Making Her Way

Three extra blankets strewn over me, & three stacks of books & notebooks next to me in bed attempting to substitute for her absence. No horizon, yet. Grey clouds, grey sea, grey earth, grey roofs, grey windows, grey hair I'm sure flying out electrically in the mirror, if I ever roust myself out of the room to take a look-see, but all I see is her making her way to Starbuck's for her caffeine fix to help get to the airport past the avalanche of scenery in Salt Lake to board Delta home. She'll probably lug the sun along with her.

Practicing for the Big Trip

> *One can say that even the most powerful, full-blooded, active personality is hardly a shadow compared to a few well-chosen words, even if they describe no more than the rising moon.* — **Czeslaw Milosz**

Both hands of my watch straight up get me thinking of my friend who vowed to shoot a picture at noon everyday for the rest of his life. Whether it's a burning sidewalk in Clearwater at noon, or dandelions erupting out of a field in Maine, or an arrow on a building in Mexico, they'll all have one thing in common, noon. A record, a photographic diary, a document. The big hand winds down the right side of the watch face past III. The bridge connecting Moon Island to Long yawns out of the fog as the ferry hits the halfway point to Boston. I put down my blue bag carrying three wise men: Lorca lilting at the moon; Kerouac howling at it; Milosz grinding his teeth in that language he's mastered with dogs snarling & barking in his distant Central European past.

I'm on the day boat to Boston practicing, gearing up for the big trip with San Francisco the destination. Little spider shimmying down her web trying to land on this notepad could get run over by the speeding scrawl of pen if she's not careful. Standing alone on the front deck, the Boston skyline cut beautifully in half by the fog. Mystic River Bridge just low enough to be seen ducking under it in the northwest. This activity, the jotting down of constant, eventual events is all I miss from my former daily commute, along with a couple of other commuters. There's a French flag unfurling above the World Trade building. A survey team where I once saw a violinist. New market umbrellas in front of the Federal Courthouse. Four young girls, ages eight to eleven, group right in front of me hoping I'll include them in the picture. They're smiling gum & braces. We're here.

Chagall's Murals for the Jewish Museum in Moscow: Love on the Stage

My first full day in town in thirty-two years, the only passenger on the Mason-Powell line this early in the morning, still essentially dark, the operator & conductor move the car down to the stop cautiously, reluctantly, it's Saturday, after all. Past the Russian Hill Market, Chinatown Public Health Center, a good view of the western arc of the Golden Gate Bridge, then the car rambling down Washington for another view of one of the bridge stanchions, Transamerica Building decapitated in fog.

What really sticks with me today is the cab ride to the San Francisco MOMA. Bearings still a little askew, & what with the Chagall Show opening today, I figure I better get there as early as possible asking the Whole Foods staff on California to call me a cab. Yellow Cab driver asks if I'm Robert before I get in. When I tell him about my earlier ride he lets me know that trolleys are a way of life where he comes from, Moscow. It's not long in the conversation, which will be limited by the distance between the grocery store & the museum, that his plaintive accent admits its Armenian. I say something about the constant hole in one's Soul that must be carried around by the displaced of that history. "Oh, you know?" he queries quietly, then goes on to say his father-in-law was a Jew, which made his wife one as well, though he doesn't allude to it, the former tortured & killed not by the Turks, but the Communists. He knows he could have made his way in Moscow. Left for San Francisco for his daughter, then three, now fourteen. In front of the museum he spells out the name of the land of his birth on a Yellow Cab Cooperative card, "Azarbaijan," turning full-face & sticking out his hand as if in some secret pact. The evidence of the hole in his Soul is in a subtle pinch of pain around the eyes, not fully released by his smile. True to his nature, drives off remaining anonymous.

Balboa Betrothed

California beckoning, again, I'm pouring over maps, guides, diaries. Examining Muir, Jeffers, Robert Louis Stevenson. Every time I look at that name on the coast, the little dot on the map, Bodega Bay, now apparently housing an aquarium, I go back thirty-two years, when heading west down that narrow road nothing could be envisioned, nothing expected, nothing known ahead of time. Yet the confidence embedded in us by so much travel must have approached, in some minor way, the built-up confidence of previous explorers, not dropping off the edge of the earth, forging ahead without trepidation. It's as if I could turn toward her now, & see the mix of fatigue & exhilaration.

Next thing I know we're on this little wharf up on aging wooden pylons housing the kind of shack with bar & restaurant, that even then was replaced all along the shores of California with Fifties kitsch. Bodega Bay. The place empty. No one. Odds are Steinbeck bellied up to this bar. A blonde came out, shy, surprised. What'll we have? Beer & menu, I guess. She could show us a menu, but they had nothing on it. The owner came out from his distractions in the back. The two of them together combined to create a low pressure center that could have caused a squall to blast through one of the open windows looking over the Pacific. Gentle, resigned to Fate, bordering on mutual depression. He made it out of Yugoslavia, somehow, found her, found this, & here they were.

I told him my own Adriatic stories of Split, Dubrovnik. He brightened up. She remained constant, her weary glow, that fading-neon resignation of abandoned dreams in California. But he picked up the pace & conversation. Animated, he said he'd get us something to eat. The two of them disappeared for a while, & came back with a mound of cold shrimp on a small bed of lettuce as gift, an offering. When was the last time, or the next for that matter, someone would carry stories of the geography of home through that door? I'd go back there next time if I thought for a moment the place still exists. I miss them. A different vantage point this time round, hating aquariums, at least the crowds around them. Bodega Bay. Pacific in memory.

The Premonitory Fog Walks Around

While she was here the sun beat down as if in love with her stretched out on the sand at Minot. Now, gone, the premonitory fog walks around without leaving a footprint. Some guy goes by me in the mist saying it's a good day for a baptism. What can one do, when all coincidences pile up, choosing a book by Olson published in San Francisco close to forty years ago printed by a guy I met in DC? It's not a book to read, but held, hand-painted woodcut for a cover, but then how can you resist a title like *Equal, That Is, to the Real Itself*, where he expounds on the impact of mass & quantity arising in the middle of the nineteenth century? Hints the vibration emanating from such structures impinging all around us can be matched by the abstract stroke of a Kline, say, or a Rothko, or language itself, if it finds a deep inherent rhythm. In two weeks I head out there, alone. Plan to keep my eyes out in North Beach, along the Embarcadero, around Chinatown, up Mission, even Nob Hill, for that matter, looking for one inch of space that hasn't been trampled, or as he puts it in the poem, "Who slays the Spanish sun…," reduced in size.

Walking San Francisco Thirty-Two Years Ago to the Present Moment

So powerful a now, that Time lifts itself up directly overhead, a bridge linking that past & near future, transubstantiating Space into distance between footsteps.

Preparations for San Francisco & Napa

In preparation for the journey West I get out my trusty sources who transform geography first-hand into words. Robert Louis Stevenson in terse prose in 1899 captures the utterly new perspective from Mount St. Helena north as far as Shasta toward Oregon; to the south San Francisco flanked by Mounts Diablo & Tamalpais; east, the eternal sea; & west the swamps & cornfields of Sacramento; finally setting sights on the earth below in Napa, & how "the soil, where it is bare, glows warm with cinnabar." From a recent history I find the word "Napa" derived from original inhabitants, the Wappo, a word itself probably an early corruption. Toward the end of his life Olson traveled out here, deciding in his little book called **West**, that the most important person he met during the reading tour through San Francisco, Berkeley, & Vancouver was "the lone Indian fishing in the Baranca del Cobre." Kerouac's record of vast discrepancies between live stones & snow on Desolation Peak, & the movie called life in the cities below: down Market Street with his big pack on his back, *hustling*, so he wouldn't bump into anyone. I go to Carl Sauer to find the source of, "The grape, out of the mountain valleys of the Caucasusis-Turkish-Iranian border lands…" Further on he theorizes that California is not settled yet, that the less deeply rooted West will continue to evolve, avoiding the Fate of a "monotonous Main Street."

Addendum

Took me two days to write "Preparations…" As soon as I finished I went back to my research. John Muir's unpublished journals made its way to one of the stacks of sources left unread. Rarely begin a book without browsing a randomness the hermetic method is familiar with. Well, there he was looking into the Vancouver woods & over Puget Sound on the very dates I wrote the above, July 20th & 21st, only, one hundred & fifteen years ago. He's fascinated by Mount Rainier & the whole Cascade Range on the 20th from Seattle at the Sound. But what does he end with? "In the foreground a red-shirted Indian in a canoe, his oars flashing silver."

The First Order of the Day

Lucky I turned around in the center of St. Helena. Pitch black, & heads & tail lights all the way down Highway 29. I had two full days left in the Valley. Already checked things out beyond the outskirts of Calistoga, but hadn't been to the town of Yountville. I made a U-turn. As soon as the center of St. Helena was behind me the same clouds covering the stars caught the first red ray of the sun shooting over the Vacca Mountain Range. Novel light above the peaks curved convex, drawing a dumb grin on the rental car driver from Massachusetts, who hadn't seen a sunrise in this Valley in thirty-two years. The vines next to Whitehall Lane Winery stretched out thirsty for a first dose of photosynthesis. Yountville beckoned, too, in silence. When I stopped in front of Gordon's Café on Washington St. I knew I was too early. But this land is work in every nook & cranny. Young twenty-one-year-old Namon was prepping with the music & the oven on. No, they weren't open for over an hour, but what did I want? Eggs & coffee? The deal was he couldn't start the brewed coffee quite yet, but big French bowls of double latté, eggs, & potatoes were the first order of the day, along with some kind of guiding, fortuitous light.

"Ah, Freedom"

There's a curved cinderblock fence painted with an ochre hue similar to the hills beyond. More than hills, I guess, the Vacca Mountains would be reduced if perspective were applied to the scene. But when I first walked out into the campus yard this morning the height the reach the nearness to the sky forced a huge sigh out, & soon followed the *choric* transformation of vibration & breath, "Ah, freedom." I breathed it in, & out, against all possible constriction.

For a Second there my Briefcase was a Leather Holster

It's bristling hot. I'm in the center of the road in Calistoga. There could very well have been a gun fight right here bullets buried under the tar. There's a literary war currently going on down the road in Napa: people trying to please each other! I just spent an hour hiding from it behind a shelf in the bookstore reading Rimbaud's **Oeuvres Complètes,** reloading my pistols just to cross the street.

Departure

That's pretty much the way I end up traveling, with tons of preparation, examining maps, documenting sources from others who lived & wrote before, scoping out bookstores & cheap eats, but not monuments, travel isn't sightseeing, but when it's time to leave, nothing, not even memorizing directions to the airport, I mean I'm on the road, living the experience, haven't time to think about departure. Walking to the airport in Belgrade in 1967 without a map, asking folks along the roads, who could only point the way. Or stranded in Mexico City, waiting for one the few responsible friends we could trust to send money left with him just in case of such a jam. Now, Napa to San Francisco International Airport at 4:00 A.M., too many bottles of wine to carry, too many shared the night before. I'll get there ok, but not before taking a wrong turn just before the right exit, ending up cruising 16th Street, & Van Ness, of all places, having to ask a bakery truck driver how to get out of the maze. At least by that time it was beginning to get light out. What really struck me was getting through Vallejo in the dark. All I could think of was Robert Louis Stevenson's comment about the place in 1880, that like a lot of California towns, the choice "was a blunder; the site has proved untenable." I was there, lost, blind, the highway interminable. It was like a dying maelstrom, or beached whale's belly. I just wanted to click my boot heels & get home.

Ordering the Waves

On the first day back from California must reconnect east. We head over to Hull, the Gut channel, the big windmill. It's one of those New England days where it's cloudy everywhere except straight up, sun burning through the cover. Walk over to the boathouse past a number of eight-man dories, red blue white, pulled up on the sand & iron rails, including *Egalite* & *Liberte*. Walk out to the end of the narrow, practically abandoned wharf, the original 4x4s keep sturdy. Eat grapes staring out toward Peddocks Island past the bridge between Moon & Long Islands toward Boston, which we could see, but for the fog. We refuse to get bogged down by the mundane. Can appreciate that, too. Climb into the *Liberte* & sail away, while stationary, like birds in a strong wind. From the oarless *Liberte* I read with pleasure *Egalite*. The ropes tying the three dories getting repairs create a double triangular pattern, ordering the waves, inviting a music.

Jettisoned

Jettisoned! That's how I continue to feel after reaching the peak of Old Toll Road in Calistoga two weeks ago to the day. Peering over the cliff edge with bodily eyes for wings, a sense of danger remaining before, & behind me. Only a few birds above. Stones rolled down. Named the grasses & weeds, yellow & red foxtail, Russian thistle. Both arroyo & agave cacti. Wind carried spirited evidence of its origins as an Indian footpath.

Back in 1880 Stevenson observed this territory as the haunt of highwaymen. At the same time, he gave credit to its vertical spurs for keeping the northern end of Napa Valley a frontier, essentially for keeping the iron horse at bay. Jettisoned, on the one hand knowing more about the grand abyss thousands of feet below, than what was ahead, ascending or descending, just a few feet around the bend. Unburdened!

Deep Association

In the dream I wore the black shirt I had on at the Napa Opera House, so that when I woke I thought I was still in bed in California planning the rest of my day. Mountains roll by on either side of me, Mayacamus to the west, Vacca, east. Stars recede back into breaking light above me, along with vineyard workers' headlights. Hot air balloons launch rainbow colors across the sky thrilling groups of tourists. The same lone cashier at Safeway will welcome me for the third straight day marveling at my papaya & Matzos. I'll head over to Napa Roasters for coffee & a table spread out with books & journals. Then I realize I'm all the way back here, a few hundred yards from the magnetic Atlantic. Illusion turns to recollection, when on the last night there, on the way back from Stag's Leap, setting sun washing color all over valley floor & hills, that image I etched permanently in memory, merged this morning with a deep association to one of van Gogh's last paintings, *The Red Vineyard*. The only one sold during his lifetime.

Love & Time Equal to Snow

It's too obvious to say, but snow simply slows things down: Time, Love, Stones. I stopped on my way to work to watch a group of glacial erratics mask themselves in a fine gauze, avatars of Strength, Mystery, Dispassion. Black umbrella above me, I studied them. Origin of renewal. Took the later ferry. Called my wife from the dock in Boston to say her face is as fresh & startling as the first time I saw her, & that I'd make the snow cave of first happiness for her, if the weather kept up. Then, on the Orange Line subway the young Asian student memorizing anatomy cards for his final exam at Tufts Dental School appeared wise with exhaustion. His wife, a hygiene student, was too empty of energy to lend an ounce of empathy, when he turned the cards around twice for answers to thorax, spinal column. Way too involved even to kiss, parting at the New England Medical stop. It's alright. After his final, after her Friday classes, they'll combine exhaustion & emptiness into a philosophy of Love & Time equal to snow, slowly exhibit qualities of character to each other like those exacted from ancient stones.

Yet Another Time to Love

Yet another Time to love. Differences in grey alone establish horizon after noon. Cruel, too, when earlier, record-breaking temperatures at dawn blew light through windows, pink, then bronze. No need for music, wind reaching siren levels, cello, or low-voiced grumbles, interpretive objections to rapid change, or loss. Another November gathering leaves ancestors often burned in piles on Broad, on Winthrop Streets, reaching back to pagan pyres, an olfactory sense emitting bliss & joy, so rare in childhood as to confound. Joy & bliss? Only, now.

V. from *Body of Time*

Since you read with your body, your body paragraphs. - **Helene Cixous**
  Three Steps on the Ladder of Writing

Even in a poem's here and now — the poem itself really has only this one unique, momentary present — even in this immediacy and nearness it lets the Other's ownmost quality speak: its time. **- Paul Celan**
  "The Meridian"

So that style is always a secret…
Its secret is recollection locked within the body of the writer. **- Roland Barthes**
  Writing Degree Zero

Symptoms of ruins. Vast buildings.
Several, one on top of the other, apartments, rooms some temples, galleries, stairways, viewpoints — fissures and cracks — I go down then climb back up. — I wonder if such a prodigious mass of stones, marbles, statues, walls, which are about to collide, will be greatly sullied by that multitude of human brains, human flesh, and shattered bones.
I see such terrible things in my dreams. **- Baudelaire**
  Notebooks

Even so, the voice consoles me: 'Keep your dreams, the wise
Have none so lovely as the mad.' **- Baudelaire**
  "The Voice"

The Physical Universe

*Once the sacred character of the body is
recognized the cosmos wheels into line.*
-Henry Miller

Wind pushing light all over the place outside. The cold another wall. Physicists now say the universe is limitless, all theory must be reformulated. Talk which ignores the substantive core of the human body is useless. Recently I picked up a book of anatomy illustrated limb by limb, organ by organ with color photographs. It's a complex, horrid mass of cells after the living skin is gone. When are you coming up to bed?

Headlines

From scratch. The mark. The body's movement up & out against the first moments of daybreak. Opening the front door, & looking for the Sunday *Times*, there's unobtrusive Jupiter, old & holding on for dear life in its wrinkled light. Searing clarity to the air. One wants to breathe only through the nose to catch the woody-scented nuances in advancing December. Two stalks of milkweed have sprung up in the corner of the front stoop of our rickety duplex. A couple of months late, in the shadows, hiding from the traffic flow that will start all too soon tomorrow, they're now spilling out furry, delicate, lacy seeds, clinging together in the cold, too late to fill the air, let alone penetrate the ground. In bathrobe & slippers, I didn't really stand out there long enough to think I'd write all this down. What I missed, ignored in my immediate observations, sensuous appreciations: two good-sized galaxies right overhead casting a long light streaming down to earth, that left there two million years ago as man began to break stones for use as tools in the Olduvi Gorge of Africa.

A Small Stone

On the second day of the Chinese New Year, Gang Liu's more talkative than ever before. They made only dumplings last night, all the ingredients folded into one means family. She won't cook whole fish, even though it could bring good fortune, it smells up the house. Her son is home from his visit to Beijing, where she is from, & where during the Cultural Revolution, when Mao called for radical change, she changed her name to a man's. Gang means steel, strength. She alludes to a recent dream of a younger man, but brushes it aside with a hand through her hair, & a laugh in the air, "Maybe in another life," going on about the Buddhist belief of coming back again. She does not. But if they are right, she'll be a stone. A small stone, not at the bottom of the sea, too cold, nor the beach, nor side of the road. Her sister-in-law wants to return as a woman, but without kids. A bad mother, Gang judges. She herself, if the belief materializes, will be a stone, a small stone, in the yard, or perhaps, with an affectionate caress of her thigh, "In my best friend's pocket."

Close Reading

Bone, skin, teeth, hair, all about to fall down or out. The rest of the organs comporting themselves as if age were extraneous. Opposing someone's gossip, or whispers of their weekly book club, I'm lining up my great ones: Dostoevsky, Nietzsche, Rilke, to see the relevance they give fracture, wrinkle, ache, loss, in a larger scheme of things. It's close to an exhumation, reading the lips of the dead, their final sighs, last articulations of life. What I've gotten from them so far is that ink & blood are nearly equal.

Purity & Mercy

No definitive reason to take the cross-town bus on the coldest day of the year, but I stood there, on Mass Ave., a long time, alone. Suddenly the wind flung a pair of lace panties sauntering clear across the road. A dance, a swagger, virgin's, prostitute's? Behind me on the Christian Science Building two carved words stared down from the cornice: PURITY - MERCY. The color of the underthings somewhere between pink & purple.

The next day on the boat above the pink-blue sea I saw newlyweds: she sat writing thank-you notes, left-handed, diamond & white gold bright. He sat mute with the curve of back I've seen only torn by ancient sculptors out of marble.

Last Train to Montpellier

In the middle of the night the diesel-fuel-blue sound of the train collided with the brilliance of the moon. She knelt up on the bed to close the storm window. Then the dream, *The Private Viewing Parlor of Kazakhstan,* could begin in peace. She told me that some of the participants in the room merely embraced. Others, she revealed shyly turning in underpants & pantyhose as she dressed for work, did more. We figured most of it was triggered by the Paris sex shop scenes Kieslowski used for backdrop in the first of his tri-color films, *Blue,* which we saw earlier that night.

Since the self-titled dream called itself "Private," I didn't hound her for details. The young woman who performed on stage in the film, wasn't she afraid her father was in the audience? Didn't she tell Juliette Binoche he glanced at his watch in order to catch the last train to Montpellier? Wouldn't my wife, whose own father died when she was three, want him to join her *anywhere,* even in the viewing *parlor?* (In French, so *to speak?*) She steps bravely into the blue Monday of work, her unresolved longing, naked, played out on the big, blue screen of grief.

Breakthrough

The fault of the stone bearing light across Time.

Tear the Flesh of Language Open

During the last week of March the end of High Street perpendicular to Atlantic Avenue, & ultimately the harbor itself, turns umbrella bone yard. One broker a wilderness lean-to in his London Fog. A female executive, wash wavering on a clothesline. One thing not under wind's control: the stone at my feet directly below the winged lion on the corner of Chadwick Lead Works. Meteorite-heavy, one side jagged granite, the other polished diorite exhumed out of Big-Dig tunnel work. All I can associate it with is Yeats's phrase, "Love is like a Lion's tooth." Love loosed upon a street in Boston. I'm going to pick it up. Tear the flesh of language open. Man straight out of the Magdalenian, using the tool, learning to talk.

Irrational as Animals

It pulled us out the door toward night, the full moon looking larger than stern red Mars, which didn't blink, & threw no heat our way, although we thought the moon just might with its column strewn across black ocean waves widening as it reached us. In fact, it did, drawing us closer together in the cool wind. Moon pulling us around in a way we couldn't bother to explain. Irrational as animals in love.

Torso

As fine a classical torso ever stumbled upon. Situated in the shop to avoid attention, rather than attract it. Small shoulder, (was it fractured on the opposite?) breasts, lithe rise of tummy to waistband above pleated skirt. Literally in awe. Same catch of breath, now, simply imagining it. Certainly sacred, & for sale. I stood there for a long time. Didn't want to know the price, nor want to know another thing than what I felt. But I knew the proprietor. Had purchased a 15th century Chinese sculpture from him years before, which although reasonable, more than that, inexpensive, took me a year to pay, a year to pick it up, tote it home, place it on the mantle. He gave me all the time I needed, worshipful, almost idolatrous time. He knew his stuff, with expert connections, an Asian partner who traveled often. Slowly, the facts came out. Sandstone, Cambodian, originally part of Ankor Wat. It was years before news of the genocide would leak out, but a shudder in my blood assured me this was not something one owned. He quoted a price, adding that a replica was also available, one from which he was sure I could never tell the difference.

Woman Married to the Sun & Wind

Though it reeks of it in that grand sequence of prose poems, **Paris Spleen**, Baudelaire uses the word prostitution only three times. He seems to equate the phenomena with generosity of spirit, a creative sharing of the self with the crowd. I suppose most of us are secretly fascinated by it, through our propensity for idealization of it as much as that for Love. In one piece of his, *The Beautiful Dorothea*, sun beats down on everyone in the seaside town. At noon dogs yelp for mercy from the heat, but Dorothea, cool in her billowing dress, as if the waft of air were a wave of water. Walking, she's working. In Nice once, as a young man, I watched my own independent like a study for weeks. Her routine, clockwork. A five-day week in fact. At 11:00 sharp she'd roll out her rattan mat on the pebbles of the public beach. Red bikini, black, white. She's etched in a young man's cortex exactly thirty-five years to this coming summer. Classically Nicoise, dark, petite, she may have come from a long line of ladies & sailors. I was always close to her on the beach. No one ever approached her there. Not a soul. She never entered the Mediterranean. Drank water, perhaps a piece of fruit. Certainly never read, but the sun, the horizon. At 1:00 she'd put her white shirt back on, gather her mat, ascend the stone stairs home. From the bar on the street she owned, I'd watch her stroll from the corner halfway down the street, then back. Many men, some as young as I, approached, talked, made offers. She was selective, or expensive, I'll never know. If I was jealous, it wasn't of the men, but of Baudelaire himself, who'd written *his* woman into history. More than speaking to her, more than touching, I wanted to transcribe her grace, her spirit that cannot be wizened with time, my anonymous woman married to the sun & wind of Nice, I desired what I have here.

Events Where They Should Be

You'll find few events where they should be: in books. It's snowing. I go out of the library without coat, hat, gloves, & stand there watching it cut through a minor stand of city pines, envelop rhododendrons underneath. Crowds pass by without a second glance. Most expressions bear this look: snow's a nuisance. Suddenly a tall African man stands right in front of me. It's Oyetokunbo, a young man I know from Nigeria, asking what I'm doing. "Enjoying the snow," is something he says he's never heard of before, walking off shaking his kerchiefed head incredulously like an oak dancing against a Northeast wind.

The Boat in the Sky Sailed Past

Restless, I got up from bed, & walked downstairs in what seemed a watery light. Troubled as much as restless, I'd wrestled with the problem for hours to no avail. Perhaps a scholarly diversion could keep my mind off a family dilemma, so I took along the book I'd been reading in order to help imagine an appropriate memorial to those lost in September, Erwin Panofsky's, *Tomb Sculpture: Its Changing Aspects from Ancient Egypt to Bernini*. I read for a while, exhausted, fretted some more over the personal crisis, then gave up. Defeated, I gave up trying to solve the problem, which only then allowed sleep like death to take over. Finally, I woke on the couch, my heart calm. I went upstairs to join my wife in bed, when through the skylight I saw the boat of Dionysos floating slowly across the sky in the watery light. I slept again, & dreamt I was driving my daughter's car, the law following me. I was ahead of the law in my daughter's white car. I knew I'd had a cup of red wine from the bottle of Coppola Rosso in the back seat. I drove on, cop car in the rear-view mirror. Entered a wooded area, & found a clearing. Shook the law off. When I woke the image of the boat in the sky, Panofsky says changed the meaning of its iconography, between 275-350 AD from "transportation to salvation," had sailed past the window frame into vast, untroubled waters.

Seaman's Identity Card

While staring wistfully toward the outer harbor, the islands, & beyond (toward Portugal & Spain) on the fast catamaran, sea spray, salt in the nose, local lobster boats dwarfed by distance, the *Nora Vittoria* suddenly slows to a crawl. I turn away toward port side where three stockbrokers, raving about an earlier 250 point surge in the market, hush up, in awe of *Rita* the tramp tanker with her Panama registry, her hull like a tight black dress, smoking, the whore, taking on all-comers: Maersk, Hanjin, Evergreen, Hapag-Lloyd. A Boston tug escorting her out like a thug pimp: $1,000 for change of structure; $1,000 for change of name; $1,000 for change in ownership; $300 for damage, $50 for extension or renewal. Visceral sadness evident in the brokers as the lady ambles slowly out of the harbor toward ports unknown. Sense a lack of freedom. After all, none owns a Seaman's Identity Card needed to board her, requiring medical certificate valid during the past two years, documentation of previous experience, & three passport photos in color. Wasn't it Freud who equated the desire for travel with desire to explore the body of a woman?

Time Ahead

Could one write it in the dark? Although I've done it, that's the question I asked when I got home, when she wasn't there yet, in the light. What I wanted to jot down quickly, without bothering to add anything more than what shown through windows, was the route the commuter ferry took outside Spectacle Island, which it rarely makes. (She's just come in in the dark, which spurs me on, dark dispersing through, no new light, but her Soul's, or body's, or both, are one?) Outside, in open water, we were no longer sheltered from onshore winds by these two hills built up in recent years by soil dug from Boston tunnel work. To that extent, "Spectacle," as Bill pointed out this morning, appearing to English settlers as a pair of eyeglasses, could now change its name, thanks to what these wonderfully industrious engineers, truck drivers, & laborers have done, (Charles Olson referred to it as the ability to "properly heap up,") to "The Mammaries." There, at the undulation of the two mounds, we passed the tanker we surely would have missed if we'd taken the normal course. Huge, blue & white, carrying DANGEROUS CARGO, the *NordEuropa* out of Helsingor. I've been to Elsinore, & I know what men want. I saw three crewmen there on the outer deck, braving the 30-knot northeast wind. But for these Vikings in sunglasses this was tropical, considering the time it takes to get from Denmark to Massachusetts, all the waves between. (You wouldn't believe how dark it's getting in here. She's preparing dinner in the dark, since I told her that is part of what this is about.) The joy on those men's faces. Port imminent. I wondered as we paralleled their path in the opposite direction what time is like now with land visible, after so long at sea with no reference point other than the abstractions of navigation, or stars too distant to be other than further abstractions? My guess is time changed. Imminence of land, of material, of the concrete, the feminine, sped things up, to the point that time, connected to sense, & against the too-long days traveled before, lay ahead for sailors with enigmatic smiles, to plunder.

Small Caps & Nasdaq Slip in Thin Trading

Dark grey sea like the pin-striped suit sitting next to me. White caps, his hair. Rain, letters, or figures in *The Wall Street Journal.* This stern Nor'easter, less threatening than even one contestant in the rat race. No information valuable enough to take with him, he leaves the paper behind in his seat. I pick it up & fold it under the soaked cover of my canvas bag hoping to keep any wit in my poems dry.

London Long Beach LA Watts Compton

My friend writes from London London's as bad as the worst American cities, drug dealers on the corners, the traffic, sounds coming from cars that make Chicago & Watts chamber music sites. He said Watts, & I'm almost there, with my radio on, driving toward the L. A. County Museum the day after 400 cops stormed the SLA secret hideout in Compton. This Revolution, televised. All day long.

If 400 cops streaming through alleys in Compton looking for four bank robbers didn't look like the Keystone '30's, I don't know what did, but this wasn't funny. I heard a few times the number of rounds fired - in the thousands. Thousands of rounds. Fired. At one house. In Compton.

Driving along, dropped out, from the world, in 1974. Watergate, so sordid, you could see the stink coming from the head of the fish running the ship of state. Thar she blew the country then, & one did well to leave. We were leaving. Waiting in Long Beach to sell the car we're in, staying with friends in Long Beach.

The only thing the woman I was with & I cared about was Patty Hearst. Hoping they wouldn't get her, at the same time wondering if they'd ever get Nixon, but not as often, & never as hard a wonder. We stopped caring about the latter, left instead. Granted, I continued to carry the transcript of the Watergate Tapes printed in the *NYT*, but after reading it, used it only to kill mosquitoes in our Mexico City hotel room.

We were on our way to the museum, for yet a third time, to see our favorite blue Picasso, the Matisse with two women seated at a table in a shady garden, Cezanne's *Still Life with Cherries and Peaches*, brilliant reds & golds in white bowls on a white cloth that ripples across the bottom like a flag. Kirchner's, *Two Dressmakers*, with knowing eyes, standing against a dazzling pink, red, lemon-yellow background.

The Beckmann we loved so much, the little prepubescent nude stood all alone up in Pasadena. We carried these colors & innocent images in our minds ahead of time, proleptically, heightened colors, dismissive colors, as yet one more form of escape, when suddenly the bulletin on the radio announced they'd found another body in the house used as the Symbionese Liberation Army hideout at 16th & something, in Compton.

What the hell street were we on when we heard it? I don't remember, that. I knew that if we drove a certain number of blocks straight ahead we'd get to 16th, & if we turned south, Compton. Our artists, including Beckmann, who hid out under the noses of his own German countrymen in a warehouse in Amsterdam could wait. We had to see this.

Watts didn't seem quite as bad as I feared. Six years after the riots, though, most of that evidence remained. But as we neared Compton, this was no remnant of a political/economic outcry from the past. This was the carnage of daily life. Squalor, destitution, imprisonment. The only two white people for a long time driving down 16th with the luxury of dropping out.

Earlier in the trip we'd been the only two whites in a grocery store in Memphis. Interesting. Made us empathize with what it must be like for the opposite to happen in Boston. Here in Compton, different, a sense of palpable violence.

Parked just outside the roadblocks. Walking toward the scene, a carnival atmosphere began, starting with a series of yard sales. People putting their belongings, mostly clothes, on the lawn, on tables, hanging from fences, in trees. Neighbors were out, talking, visiting, smiling, music blasting, a far cry from the previous 20 blocks before we got there.

The usual camera crews, but most gone. The all-day day-before coverage was all the news stations needed to replay. It was over. Yet, just hours before that they'd found another body, in the house used as hideout. A female. Charred & unrecognizable. Just then, we turned the corner to the scene, an empty space.

An empty space in the middle of all these houses constructed exactly alike, little four-room boxes. Surrounding the empty space, four burned out houses, just shells, nothing inside. The empty space was a curious thing. How could something, a structure, a replica of all we'd seen while driving for the past three-quarters of an hour, just disappear?

If they found a body there two hours ago, how could a body be found in an empty space? We were wondering. It seemed an optical illusion. We thought the radio said, "found in the house." But now that we looked at it, we remembered it said, "cellar of the house," & now with the bulldozer heaping debris & rubble over the hole that was the cellar, where there is no cellar to what is no house.

We walked where we could, put our thumbs in bullet holes in the sides of houses just as we'd done earlier in the trip in Philadelphia, into holes Rodin tore out for the eyes of his sculpture of Balzac. Huge holes. Who was in the cellar that no longer was? Empty space. An end. A "The End" down the street from the film illusion, Hollywood.

More reason than ever to get out of town. Out of the contiguous 48. Let's drop the price of the car. Let's hope it isn't Patty. Let's go see the paintings. I remember her name, even now, the anonymous corpse America resembles now & again, but somehow regains its name, Camilla Hall.

Zen February: Coltrane Piece

> *One of the most baffling things about America is that despite its essentially vile profile, so much beauty continues to exist here.*
> **-Amiri Baraka**

That fine orgasmic tone, that screechy, animal timbre of terror & potency, percussive bloodlines, sonic knivings, guttural cuts, the great place the throat can summon the soul up from, & the ultimate rancor of death. Coltrane's heart, lung, pain, on the last Paris tour in '65 with Jimmy Garrison arcing bow across bass for angular sound on *Blue Valse* as well as any Casals or Ma. Jazz history has Elvin Jones storming off stage, angry, emptying a trunk full of drum paraphernalia onto the floor as if it were War. Garrison improvising cover. John Cage said he'd be content with black rectangles & squares, provided Rauschenberg painted them.

Aegean Shimmering

> *When one returns from the voyage one longs for the wines of Samos.* - **Cavafy**

I disembarked at Boston Harbor today, the sun so brilliant, & a new lower angle across the water, essentially ALL LIGHT, made me think of the Aegean, & what it would be like to be there for a long time with nothing to do but write. So I diverged around, lollygagged really, around the waterfront just soaking in the goodness, & struggling to make that goodness there, in the present space, in spite of what we take for granted in America, or having to be in this culture, Wall Street, the Rat Race, but fearing, too, that if I had nothing to do but write, I very well may not be able to, on an anonymous road, in a small town, in Greece, say, on Samos, for example. Then, on a bench, a woman in black, sat with a ten-x-five-inch writing pad open on her lap. Pencil in hand. Tanned. Wizened. Hair kept in a black net. On the page I could make out a scrawl, on all the worn pages sort of stacked up, but over the scrawl on each line, each line divided down the middle set up by the writing pad, every line & words underneath covered over by exquisite cross-outs, arcs of graphite shining on the greenish paper against the gold sun. I was stunned. She had all the time in the world to write, this street person getting on fifty years old, everything she'd written written over with the slashing, contradicting sharpness, or dullness, of her pencil. It had the look of an abacus, a word from the Hebrew for a drawing board covered with dust, from *abhaq*, dust. What was she accounting for, tolling, mourning the death of language? After the briefest eye contact, a minor smile, I moved on, only to turn back to watch her look down at the pad, not writing, yet, but with her other hand taking a drag from her cigarette. I walked away with my imagined Aegean shimmering in the distance, in desire, & trepidation.

(*This experience took place on the morning of September 11th, at around 7:45 A.M., as she & I looked out on Boston Harbor, Logan Airport in the distance. A draft was completed just as a colleague reported news of the first plane's crash.*)

Everything is Marked

The massive, white, *Europa*, sailing back to Nassau out of Boston Harbor right next to Logan Airport exactly two weeks to the day after the Towers fell. Escorted starboard, port, stern & bow, by four Coast Guard boats armed with .60 caliber machine guns mounted on deck. A gray day accentuating its glacial size. It should have been an awesome sight. One of the boats sped up between our commuter ferry & the cruise ship making me realize that no other craft would get between her & her escorts, not even the Outward Bound kids in their launch. It should have been impressive. But then I looked up to the third deck of the luxury liner & saw pairs of terrycloth-robed passengers, two-by-two, each looking through mini-cams, recording the scene for folks back home.

I started to imagine what kind of narrative could accompany the sight of camouflaged soldiers (neighbors would never see the white terrycloth), (my friend David had written that morning of the million dead at Stalingrad), taped voices attempting to heighten the drama of their videos, forcing everyone back home to think that when they were here in Boston they were at the Front, in the War on Terrorism. Who could stomach the idea of being subjected to any of those home movies? Worse, why weren't more passengers out on the decks? Eating in the myriad of dining rooms.

Disembarking, I asked one of my fellow commuters, a mere acquaintance, "How are you?" His answer rang as hollow, & flat as my inquiry, so that I had to add, "Everything is marked by what happened two weeks ago today."

Today I Want to Shape it a Bit Differently

I love the new reconstruction of the seawall. Two cranes at it all summer. Shoring up the wall with huge glacial erratics, a few indigenous to the area, but you can tell most have been trucked in from points North & West. I love the niche I've discovered, where I can disappear to an entire continent, & stare out worshiping, studying the sea. My first thought when I saw it was, "It's a *mihrab*," the single alcove built into the walls of churches in Byzantium. That would be a cool thing to do, wouldn't it? To write down everything that goes on all the time, it's so filled with life. The tanker balancing on the horizon line, the two diving cormorants in the foreground, the spider underneath me mapping the labyrinth. Motors & wind & waves. I suppose it would end up the *New York Times*. I equate myself with the brick maker. The prose poem of mud & straw & blood. Quite simple. Reliable. Useful in numbers, & formidable when thrown through a plate-glass window. But today I want to shape it just a bit differently. Still humble, but elevated. Knowing full-well this medium was not held in high esteem, & that Origen, or Apollonius, put down the chosen material as crass in comparison to gold & ivory, today I want to leave the equivalent of a terracotta figure here in the stone niche. I'm gathering clay with a spade & hod from one of the numerous beds around Crete. I know that during the Mycenaean Period the industry was so vast that each statue sold cheap. That suits the prose poem, the brick, for that matter, just fine. After molding it in my margins, & adding some tempera colors: black red yellow blue green, all I have to do is fire it to between 750 & 950 degrees. Have you felt a poet's desire? Cool down, my little Sapphic Aphrodite, cool down in this contemporary wind. Humble image of Love, rise out of rhythm in these waves, stand straight,

& tall, try not to crack a smile in clay at the recollection here, of Sappho in the ecstatic verbal ejaculation of her ardor, promising to sacrifice a white goat at your altar!

How Far Back Does Desire Reach?

Onshore wind producing excavating waves revealing stones unseen for years. Desire & light. Ancient desire. Desire reaching back to the oldest image of boats on Aegean seals: high prow forging over spiraled water, low stern, keel projecting beyond. Square sail. Vessels capable of voyages from the Cyclades or Crete to Syria & Egypt. A world washed in new light. From the beginning I wanted to turn the object of my desire (my wife), into the image of a small boat. Lacking technical skills, but not desire. How far back does desire reach? Desire born of the marriage of Night & Day. Not excessive desire, which kills desire. The image of a small boat, her ribs into those of a canoe, say. Then one morning in 1946, the year I was born, George Seferis, after chopping wood, swimming, watched a fisherman pass, who offered fish from his boat he called a *kourita*. He was from Asia Minor. The boat originated in Smyrna. The beautiful old wood, the carving on prow & stern recalling icons from the past. He observed this boat with much joy. Poem of desire. A small boat, her ribs. This image based on the sculpted stone *kourai*, whose sail is the carved *chiton* lifting her body. The sailor riding the image of the memory of the woman until he returns to the real thing. Ultimately reminding one of the other stone boat: the foundation plinth for Nike of Samothrace at the top of the staircase in the Louvre!

How to Get it Out!

Take Euripides down to the sea. Horde of Bakkhai, wind swirling around waves & stones like a wild animal, choric utterance welling up with what it finds down there under the surface below the rational. That's just it: getting the words down. Down to where the blood is, the viscera, one must follow in the footsteps of the Maenads, follow Dionysos down to the *temenos*, where Karoly Kerenyi got it right, saying the god of the irrational will always do the one thing required of him when he sets foot on sacred ground: commit sacrilege! The only greater desire for her is desire to praise her.

Self-Portrait, after Rilke

Indifference is that luxury never afforded him, but for briefest reverie, a blink. Long bevy of ancestors congregating behind intensity of eye. The photo shows a survivor of war, evident in scars. Sex is there, streaming from below. The whole body welling up: rhythmic lung; liver pushed to the brink; thorax & torso nothing short of voracious; heart, sturdy as a stone mason, or as compassionate as a French grandmother after midnight mass, or occasionally, ruthless as father's. Knowledge appears at the level of the simplicity of work, complexity of words. Living spent in the realm of pure moment. The lens summed it up in an instant. Intuitive, tactile nature, ready to form yet another sentence, as if later, death is articulate.

Learning Joyously Learning

Days may be growing shorter, but this renewed, instantaneous, morning light, celebratory & red over the water, as if the dome of the Pantheon were modeled on earth's architectural attachment to the sky. But work takes us underground. Dirt's one thing. Filth, another. Walls of the Orange Line at the State Street stop could very well be leprous with electrical detritus. Let's put it this way: it's no Valencia de Alcantara, Spain! So I reel back in my imagination, close olfactory receptors, squint, until one stop later, at Downtown Crossing, the gorgeous aural takes over as doors open & the live sound of The Temptations' *My Girl* flows into the car out of the mouth of a guy my age. More Chicago in that hat than Boston. It's a baby carriage in front of him wheels whatever powers that lone amplified speaker clearly modulating a fine electric guitar, not just covering the song, but brilliantly interpreting it, so that when I turn around with a smile to catch as much as I can, I see a row of five adolescent young men sitting on the wooden subway bench, as close to the musician as possible, digging the archetypal rhythm, swaying, goofing, learning, joyously learning twelve days before Christmas, when being on time for school is their last priority in the world.

The Man with Two Souls

Two things about that one thing: I knew a man, who in an intolerably insomniac state begged for a moment's sleep, fell off for about ten minutes, during which time, dreamt he'd grown another scrotum. Amazed, he showed both to a few friends from adolescence. They burst out laughing causing him to burst out laughing, waking himself up in a giddy Freudian Joy!

In 1914, while staying in the newspaper office of Apollinaire, the Italian Futurist, Carlo Carra, created a collage made of tempera, newspaper, & white paint on cardboard titled, *Free-Word Painting -Patriotic Celebration*. Its first two words: "SUN SCROTUM"!

Nativity with Dance

for **Kathleen** *&* **Karen**
Thea & **Avry**, *& of course* **Nana**

A single surge of love occurred, less than momentary, it could have been lost if I weren't used to paying attention to such subtle internal sunbursts. Just a curve in the road, & blam, her birth. In four days we'll celebrate the ritual of the return of the day of her birth. That quarter-second flash shot forth associations of nativity with dance. Granted, Coltrane chanted minutes before, "A Love Supreme, A Love Supreme, A Love Supreme, A Love Supreme, A Love Supreme," & granted, I connected it to the time Joe Schuyler first turned me on to it, naively thinking then how beautifully romantic a piece it was instead of the spiritual thrust Coltrane aimed at. Also recalled the time I met Judith Jamison of the Alvin Ailey American Dance Theater on 7th Street in DC, when we shook hands, & talked about ambition & dance, but yes, when the flash blam of love surged concerning her birth, I thought, too, of her recent revelation that the day before that event her mother was on the dance floor at the reception of her own brother's wedding, jitterbugging with the best of them, the rest of them you might say, *not with child*, & as she said, "The next day the twins dropped out."

I figure the twins came out dancing, because to this day she's about the best I know, outside of Judith Jamison in her prime. The time in Cannes the guys were falling all over themselves to join her. The times we're alone, under the influence of wine, pairing up, & off she makes moves no choreographer has yet recorded, kinesthetically responding to my hyperactive jolts which look more like pugilism than dance, & she is black in the dark with the jazz on reaching everyone's shared African roots shaking into a state of movement alone, to the extent that I thought of her again a few miles down the road when the green heron soared over wharf rooftops, a bird I could identify in the grey sky not from any noticeable color, but from strength of wing-beat, through its actions alone.

Convulsive Beauty

Convulsed. The word came up from the body's depths, rather than anything cerebral. Of course, the word Beauty followed shortly after, something thought about, associated as it is with Breton's theory of how Beauty will, or will not be. Sea roils now. In the dream last night the *tsunami* rose slowly to a height of thirty feet. I was in the water trying to draw others' attention to it. At the top, fringes of foam hung like Hokusai's *Great Wave*. I could turn & walk to shore if I wanted to, but in the dream my calm expectation was equal to the possible appearance of the Goddess of Love stepping from behind the curtain of water, as if it were a stage, or as it is now, waiting for her to emerge from behind the bathroom door, not yet dressed for the workday ahead.

Drawings for Dante's Inferno

Hell, not at the margins, but in the main. The drawings required a plodding, deliberate Canto-by-Canto reading, yet each exhibit the quick, spontaneous brilliance of Rauschenberg's genius: "My hands are one step beyond my head... reaching for contact." One can't hover above the crater of Hell as witness, but must descend. Is it, can we blame it on the world's overpopulation that Hell itself has risen? There are fissures in the earth where the damned appear, & now through no fault of their own, *(there is no room in Hell,)* the people of Srebrenica reveal themselves, having lived on nothing for the past year except for pear-tree bark & mountain snow. One can't excavate the laws of Hell, who cries, "Mama & Dada!"

When Time is No Solution

That's exactly what I'm doing today, walking around in my head, not surprised to find that the letter "L" shaped like a leg rose up 3,000 years ago out of Palestine. Head. Dark corridors. Cul-de-sac. Myriad stones strewn over the open road. It's frightening when time is no solution. Last night she dreamt we bought a huge console clock at an estate sale. When carrying it out, jewels suddenly appeared on the wooden case. But today the quality of personal time is no consolation. There are men who love war. She told me last week she stumbled upon "labyrinth" in the dictionary, close to the word "labia." Absence of woman is a cause of war. The current political landscape of Palestine is a time without presence, covered with men without legs to stand on, a territory like the labyrinth, ancient enigma named after the double ax.

To Breathe the Least Bit of Fresh Air

On the fifth day of summer in the middle of the afternoon under a stone lion sweating the last of its magma steam the young woman from Martinique eased into shadows of buildings as if they were the shade of trees, then disappeared before northern eyes. The tailor of the men's clothing store, *Ari*, stepped out for a moment with a thread on his pants, a thread on his jacket, which he removed, both threads spinning him around until he must have stood there on the sidewalk, naked & cool. The woman reappeared out of the brick, out of the granite in her dress of blue water. In the parking lot of *Il Panino* a waiter left orange peels on the hood of his Volvo, while talking with two women, adding a sense of green absent from the pavement. Yet amid all this Peace, this collection of habits from home, the harsh reality of trouble underground, back on the subway where four Jewish kids with tennis rackets strewn all over the car floor talked in front of a man reading the Koran, the man reserving an extra seat for the Koran, & glances of hate tossed at the boy in the yarmulke, which I witnessed when he tried to stare me down but my eyes wouldn't lower, & all three Gods, adamant in the corner of the car couldn't devise a way to breathe the least bit of fresh air into a sticky political situation.

First TV Appearance

The cabby knew right away 5 Penn Plaza translated into the CNN building. My wife prepared nervously for days for her first TV appearance, "live." We confirmed our identities at the desk, headed up to the 20th floor. After signing in again, Chantal, with the look & demeanor of generations from the society pages, greeted us. Straight to make-up, my wife turned camera ready. I watched from the monitor. A barrage of unrehearsed questions on taxes. True poise, real expertise. When it was over she recalled it as a blur, but was ecstatic. Even managed to give the moderator a résumé from her daughter, who wants to be an anchor. Went back to our room where they put us up at the Waldorf. My earlier wine excursion had a bottle of Veuve waiting on the windowsill in a plastic bag of ice. No need to mention the name of the French restaurant where we'd made reservations, but I will introduce here, Thierry, our waiter, proud of his Brittany heritage, proud of his boys speaking both French & English, doing so well in school, his determination to return at some point, open his own establishment. I'll add the heavy tip, as well, for apart from praising her yet again for her beauty & competence, the point of all this is as contrast to the harsher reality about NYC, an image starker than anything reported via the once or twice removed medium of television. At 545 East 55th Street, under some scaffolding jutting onto the pavement, two human legs, rat-like, but weary, crawled into the cardboard front door of his shelter, a current of frigid water running around & under it, an image that didn't allow us to continue on immune from pain.

Simone

Displacement written on her face, across the room, wallflower with no one to talk to among the large group of people. A gathering, one of those department parties when someone has made a break from the uneven circle of work, & though everyone is invited the power points are distributed around the room, condescension prevented from filtering too low, Simone, the Temp, is left to fend for herself.

The Dean's this, the Dean's wife that. The roles & the reams. It's nothing but shop. Some quip about computers virtualizing the mind's fantasy, a doctor's wish writing will come to.

Simone nods across the vast desert of the room like a black-eyed flower touched by a sudden wind. Of recognition. Attracted to that as matter is to the black absence of space, I mistake her for French. She's from Iran. Petite & past her prime, but not yet as wizened as the Marguerite Duras of photos. She reminisces of Paris & Teheran, praises the heightened sensitivity of the French, the poetic nature of Persians embodied by Omar Khayyam & Rumi. Recites in Farsi a poem about wine jugs broken on the ground by the wind & anger turning the poet's face black, translating it stanza by stanza to English. Glowing like an orange tree, while speaking Farsi, she quiets, whispers me closer as if offering a gift. One, looking around, she refuses to share with those who've ignored her.

There was an old woman she was very fond of, a Jew, the whisper went, who as a young girl in the Warsaw Ghetto was allotted bread only every three days. To ward off the intervening hunger, she placed a few pieces in a can & buried it outside. She kept it full this way. The beautiful postponement young girls are wont to. One day during an especially intense bombing the earth let go, the hidden sustenance disappeared.

Simone wants to share the lesson of the story, but displacement returns. Her language, ensnared in a net of cultures, forces her to tell me the old women advised her, "Endure the moment," rather than as she later said she meant to say, "Enjoy, of course."

Can You Get a Sense of the Weight of a Gun From The Movies?

The day before we praise warriors in November, leaves from adolescent trees on the sidewalk on Mass. Ave. look as if stars fell overnight. In mourning. Kids in Kosovo, just north of the Cursed Mountains already curtained with snow, warm hands over steel boxes half-full of coals. It's reported the enemy took a motor from a sewing machine as an imbecilic act of sabotage, threw porcelain cups out of a school window with the genius velocity of light. I know of a young female runner made of bronze in 560 BC found in Albania. Why is she looking backward with such trepidation? Why lift her skirt to keep it from getting entangled at the knee? Why one breast out from tunic? How far are the Balkans from the strife of ancient times?

Elliptical, Cryptic Fragments Stand in for Entire Philosophical Tracts

Needed to find a secret place equating itself with a sense of freedom. It had to be brand new. Even with the newly discovered, recently bloomed mimosa in the neighbor's yard out the back window, oppression at home, created by a fissure of children, obsessive obligations, manipulative guilt married into, turned me out, forced me to look elsewhere to figure out a dynamic problem without rational solution. The last sentence is as stupid as the dog constantly barking two streets over today, & doesn't come close to defining the dilemma.

I packed a few books, a bottle of Bordeaux, waxed-paper cups. Drove ahead. Thought ahead, north. Didn't really want to be away long, or leave her. Constricted chest loosening with each mile. Made a sharp turn. A right turn, it turns out. I eased toward the sea, inching slowly downward toward sea-level.

God, when I saw the cliff in the near distance jutting above the road, man, that majesty meant freedom. Shortly I realized it was part of an island across the channel at the tip of the peninsula. A few cars parked as close to the water as they wanted. No **No Parking** signs.

I shut the engine off. Watched water flow, cliff stand tall. Locked the car, & walked. That rhyme's as dumb as the two dogs barking back & forth out there past the fading mimosa. Williams once wrote that his work aimed, "to reconcile the people & the stones." Felt that there. Grey stones, words, green, white lines, microcosmoses.

At the end of the strand I turned away from all civilization except previous ones. Lone figure at the low-tide mark bent gathering something. Here, the idea of freedom surfaced. From or of? Half-way down a man entered at the previous division of civilizations, carrying a child. Asian. Instinctively, I knew he was linked to the figure gathering seaweed or mussels in the distance.

I'm home. Free. Not of, but from. If that answer seems elliptical, or cryptic, I can only recommend finding a secret place, where elliptical, cryptic fragments can stand in for entire philosophical tracts, or lifelong analysis. The lone dog now barking varies its monotonous tone. The screechy squeals it's reaching must be a mere plea for freedom. However twisted, anguished.

In the Remotest Mansions of the Blood

> *But one must awaken the duende in the remotest mansions of the blood.* **- Lorca**

It was brief, the last dream of night, turned morning. The scene suspect from the start. A dark, cellar-like, or cave-like chamber. The confusing image of a victim of sacrifice. At first, the sense of film, or staging. Upon reflection it was straight out of the black paint pots & palette of Ribera. Long black hair, arms strung upright in ropes, naked. The slender body revealing a straight line of hair at the pubis, cut & shaped like a stripper's. Very suspect. My dream eyes traveled up from loins to chest - no breasts. No young face, either, to match the sex as presented. Slowly the male face revealed itself in movement - a look toward his torturers as they approached, whose approach, reproached. Three men grabbed his chest & loins from behind suddenly producing lemon-sized breasts, which bled when they squeezed. The little (androgynous) penis that surfaced in place of the female pubis bled a black, oily blood, as the Lorcan ecstatic smiled at the pain & production of red & black colors defying every intention of the captors.

That Most Melancholic of Bach

From the balcony I could see the stone bridge solidly marking the time when they named such structures after poets. Pursuing ecstasy through excess I took my last glass of Port out there where city lights rivaled the stars. Inside the hotel room the dream waited like the skin of a woman so pellucid one could see into her flesh. *Komm, süsser Tod*, that most melancholic piece by Bach we listened to earlier, recorded in Barcelona by Pablo Casals, who died thirty years ago today, must have invited the orchestra into the hotel lobby of the dream.

Its conductor showed me the program for the upcoming fall concert, pointing out minor flaws in the music, (resounding through corridors), which had to be ironed out before then.

They asked me to tell the young man just sitting down to the harpsichord at the far end of one wall, that the instrument belonged to them, not the hotel. Letting him know, I told him how difficult it was for me once when they kept me from writing on my computer at work. I'd never spoken that gently to another human being in real life, with the sole possible exception of my wife. I crossed further thresholds & passageways as pellucid as skin one could see through.

The Music & Art of a Friend in Vienna

Somebody's making a racket across the street, saws, lawnmowers, not important enough to go to the window to investigate. Your niece just knocked on the study door to say she's headed off to work at the TV station in Boston, but not before stopping off at the gym, & calculating what her new salary breaks down to, what with overtime on Saturdays, figures she's going to make out all right. We signed one of your sisters up for email newsletters from the Musikverein there in Vienna so that maybe she & her twin can take in a concert when they visit you in December. They don't list the hospital you went into this morning for pre-op on the inner city map that cites the museum with the bulk of the world's Bruegels, & that Rembrandt *Self-Portrait* in which he stares the beginning of his economic struggles square in the face lit by some sacrosanct mixture of ochre pigment & courage.

On the Day that I Met Him

Find oneself lost in that goofed, lone world of solitude, even with others around, commuting even, head in a book, say, when someone out of pure politeness & social grace, asks, "How are you?" Look up & see the friendly face smiling. Instead of responding in a sane, normal manner, "Well Nietzsche said suicide can get one through many a bad night. This cold had me thinking all night of taking the day off, but here I am going in anyway." That's all one needs to start the day: Nietzsche & suicide uttered to a stranger before 8:00 in the morning. But that's how I met Herman Zinter, whom I caught up with to apologize, once out of that previous world. Turns out he teaches architecture. Turns out we stand under the winged lion of my favorite building in Boston. He's headed to breakfast, which jolts his memory of Joyce's chapter in **Ulysses** linking architecture & food. We shake hands. What are the chances?

At one o'clock Bloom orders a glass of good Burgundy at Davy Byrne's Pub. He wonders whether his hunger is pleasure or pain. Orders a cheese sandwich with Italian olives, added. Wine burns his & Joyce's curiosity about the curiosity of food. Who opened & ate the first oyster? It took the French to invent a needle for eating periwinkles. I ordered a fresh salmon sandwich at Byrne's Pub in 1981. The sun in the Burgundy drives his memory to Howth. Lion's Head is a promontory on the southeastern side of Howth. Yeats watched the white birds there with Maud Gonne. Molly, supine above earwigs in the sedge, feeds Bloom the chewed seedcake from her mouth to which Bloom responds, "Joy: I ate it: joy." He's on his way to the National Library, which he thinks was designed by Sir Thomas Deane, architect of the Trinity College Museum, & the Ruskin Museum at Oxford. Herman Zinter is engaged to Helen White, whom he kissed, on the corner of High St. & Batterymarch, on the day that I met him.

Toward the Center

It's a longing. One bred out of times I can't be content in the moment, either the joy of it, or the boredom, rarely, or suffering it. So out! Need to travel. But can't, because of circumstance: the job; normal constrictions; lack of total freedom. Who has that anyway? So who's going to drive me back to the moment, erase the wretched longing? Landscape pages of a book can be traversed. A rereading? I could go with Walter Benjamin's minute description, under the influence of hashish, of Marseille. Cross country via Kerouac. This time I want to be the donkey walking next to D. H. Lawrence in Italy. I choose Sorgono. I want his impression. Lawrence, the man who always seemed so wise, vigorous, a pantheist, really loving Nature, loving man & woman only close to Nature. Didn't Birkin say in **Women in Love**, he could care less if the whole race disappeared, & earth return to grass & rabbits? Lawrence, almost Darwinian in his choices of the few fit enough to survive his law, his ethic. Lawrence dead at 44, the damned shame, I could read so much more. The train winds like a snake up the hills out of Mandas to Sorgono in the middle of Sardinia. He jots down the trees, the hazels, myrtles, arbutus scrub. But he doesn't miss judging the quality of Sardinian coal, which he finds soft, not fit for steam, dirty. Trees are naked. He'd paint the brown cork trees as if they were Tahitian girls! He desires tree-speech! A fig tree walks up to him in her nudity. Maybe that's where he got his poem *Figs*, "The Italians vulgarly say, it stands for the female part; the fig-fruit; the fissure, the yoni, the wonderful conductivity toward the center." His respect for peasants in the distance, comparing them to oxen, goats, never abandoning their defenses, stern as badgers Lawrence totes his **Baedecker**, but it's outdated. Chosen hotel gone. The only remaining inn is filthy. It's one thing for farmers, shepherds tracking dirt, but clean sheets are essential. He's afraid his own boots are cleaner than the stained bed he's shown. He furies. He walks out. He & his wife find themselves in the middle of a public lavatory. The mountain air is frigid. Does the author ever eat? It's a seven-hour train ride got them here. He climbs up. Part of the knot of mountains known as Gennargentu. He's suddenly Gerald Crich at the end of **Women in Love** abandoning everything human for pure death offered by snow. But his wife is with him, he has to turn around. At the inn there will be no milk till seven, no food till seven, no fire. He trudges out, again. He watches sunset. He begins to understand his black rage is caused by his *expectations* of Sorgono. I begin to cast off my desire to flee, finally drop my desire for future cities, imagined Malta, Palermo, Tunis. I'm here, at work, within.

Crossroads

Sea smoke in the distance, ax close at hand. Stood at the crossroads, which rose up before me. The roads rose up. Looked both ways, forward & back, both ways, left & right, both ways, up & down, & chose the path, which led me here.

Venice via Hell & Belgrade

Mere mention of Venice calls up memory fragments of just getting there. I was twenty. On the bus in Munich Charlotte Appleton's hair flashed like a stoplight. Avoiding another's clutches she sat down next to me. We slept that night fully-clothed in a park under honeysuckle. She was from California, had an abortion earlier in the year, sent to Europe by her parents to forget. The first girl I ever met on the pill. She was headed to Greece. What coincidence! Travel together, down the Adriatic, hitchhike our way through Yugoslavia.

"Passports!, passports!, passports!," the chorus of armed soldiers ringing above drumming boot heels after crossing the Austrian border by train at Ljubljana. Darkness a palpable force. My heart a vessel of trepidation. Disembarking at Rijeka. Who told us we could make it to Split for $5 sleeping on deck the mail boat? Twelve hours later, the Adriatic at Split miraculously clear where we waded. From the promontory cliff we witnessed the circular turn of celestial time, full moon rising opposite setting sun. Earth one huge room.

My immense ignorance knew it was four or fourteen hours by bus to Belgrade. Fourteen hours to Belgrade. Turn-of-the-last-century sights along the way: wooden ploughs; faggots stacked high on a man's back permanently bent; homemade clothes; the modern world a rumor. Between bus & train station, truck depot, we found the only room in town. $1.25 a night overlooking a soccer field where workers gathered to play in the afternoon, & once a man emerged from the door in the concrete bleachers with his family, their home. With eight single beds in the room, we waited for the other guests who never showed.

Every morning for over a week we walked to the outskirts of town, thumbs out, only to be mocked by fingers mimicking scissors cutting hair. Stuck in the *cul-de-sac* of Belgrade, surrounding states of Albania, Romania, Bulgaria, black holes in the constellation of nations. Darkness, an ominous force. Too much truth in the dog-eared copy of Fromm's, *Escape from Freedom*. My heart breaks at the recent atrocities, told & untolled rapes, less-than animal cruelties at Omarska, Srebrenica, Tuzla. Viscera eviscerated. I'm not sure an ounce of courage existed without the presence of Charlotte.

Which way to turn, but up? Sky, the luxury. Let's say it was $37 for two one-way tickets to Venice, the quickest way out, Belgrade clinging like a caul to the stillborn artist & Charlotte Appleton of California. We walked all day to the airport. Slept all night in the terminal. Thirty years ago, can't recall boarding. The relief of air - feet off the ground. One stop, a last, brief look at Dubrovnik, it's beautiful walled-in orange roofs. Then Venice, all aboveboard. Canaletto, spatial contemporary of Fitz Hugh Lane. Venice, nothing but light. Charlotte made it to Greece from Rome.

Venice, contrasting light, vivid as freedom, or being alone.

A Last Reminder

Last day of winter won't disappoint. Rain one degree from the gentleness of snow rides the added chill of March wind bruising skin blue, or red, dreary, dismal. Olson called it dour. You'd have to be touched to want 70 degrees, & giddiness. Give us all a last reminder of how we're going to spend the bulk of our days. Pretty dark down there, & dank. Out there in the distance at the tip of the Hull peninsula, the new-age windmill is a single prop-engine ready to take off, but the sky above & behind it is pure Dutch, pure Jacob van Ruisdael. This sea's not as rough as his rough seas, but the clouds are as good as his nautical views, matching even the best ones, those premonitory clouds of *The Jewish Cemetery*. Tomorrow at 2:16 in the afternoon at the equinox we can smile a smile of glee & optimism, but until then let's stay in the character of the season.

Three Liberating Dreams

Late sunrise. Black water. That's all of today I can bear. Those shallows, before I dredge up dreams at mid-week. How spectacular the joys she described as children on the stage of her dream unfurled a cloth strung between two poles, a multi-colored rainbow, the image of her daughters' newly-found freedom. The ecstatic smile she had reporting it. That same night I had a young woman appear to me saying I was sensitive as a child. Then I dreamt of interpreting the dream of a plane flying over a city, knowing it was Baghdad, the plane toting votive candles instead of bombs, portraying my wish the threat of war melt away with Time.

Diving Through the Other Side of Time

Thankful to my ancient dream-makers for the early morning April 21st image of the river gods emerging human. It was a long canoe ride with an old master, a coach, who'd become a wine store owner. He wanted to fire my friend Greg for giving me a bottle of red wine while he worked at his store. I said, "Look, Alex, I can't recall him doing that more than three times." Now, Alex remained adamant. He'd just given me a bottle of wine, also, which is how all this came up, I mean I hesitated to take a second gift of wine from the same source in one night.

On land Alex would have none of it, no pleading would budge him, but here, on the river rapids, the spray, the risk, he had on his waterproof gear, yellow & blue, hell, he was open to anything & saw no harm in the gift from Greg. He's still a hero of mine, Alex Kulevich. Somehow the dream orchestrated a way for me to scale the high cliffs. Along the black iron railing, which paralleled the lofty ledge, while I was safely on the landward side, women in black straddled their way out along the edge.

When I looked down the river was clear. Naked bodies visible, swimming below. I saw divers at every height, from the top of the other side, to various points in between. Here's the ancient image one can't see outside the dream. (Unless it's Juliette Binoche swinging in the chapel air among the fresco figures of Piero della Francesca's cycle of the *Legend of the True Cross* in *The English Patient*.) I am marveling at the paradisiacal scene. The real archetype intervenes. A young man, he could have been a boy, crouches in the rectangle carved in the middle of the ravine across the way. I know he's going to dive, but he looks up. Did he look my way?

My dilemma, the discrepancy in this loss of logic taking place within the dream is, "Why would he dive into the river if he has those wings to soar?" There he is, white cloth swaddling his midriff, getting ready to make a move, white wings apparently attached to his back. He dives. What remains within the carved niche is an ancient *bas-relief* of off-white marble wings. The wings weren't his, but of his lineage.